Praise for *Midnights with the Mystic*

"No lofty thoughts, just the truth. Cheryl Simone and Sadhguru
not only tell it like it is, they show us how make use of this
information to expand, enjoy, and appreciate our lives."
—Dr Joe Vitale, author of *The Attractor Factor* and *The Key*

"Extraordinary wisdom, the insight and clarity of logic, the
language of a poet. If you read this powerful book, you
will discover who you really are, who we all are."
—Neale Donald Walsch, author of *Conversations with God*

"When you read this book, I know you'll resonate with its
truths, be touched in ways that can trigger your own
transformation, and realize, as I have, that a peaceful, fulfilling,
and vibrant life is available for one and all who open themselves
to receive the abundant Grace of this unparalleled being."
—Richard from Texas (from *Eat, Pray, Love*)

MIDNIGHTS WITH THE MYSTIC

A LITTLE GUIDE TO FREEDOM AND BLISS

CHERYL SIMONE AND

SADHGURU JAGGI VASUDEV

HAMPTON ROADS
PUBLISHING COMPANY, INC.

Cover design by Kathryn Sky-Peck
Cover photographs by Getty Images

Hampton Roads Publishing Company, Inc.
1125 Stoney Ridge Road
Charlottesville, VA 22902

434-296-2772 • fax: 434-296-5096
e-mail: hrpc@hrpub.com • www.hrpub.com

If you are unable to order this book from your local
bookseller, you may order directly from the publisher.
Call 1-800-766-8009, toll-free.

Library of Congress Cataloging-in-Publication Data

Simone, Cheryl, 1953-
Midnights with the mystic : a little guide to freedom and
bliss / Cheryl Simone with Sadhguru Jaggi Vasudev.
    p. cm.
    Summary: "A personal recounting of the author's five-day
retreat with her guru, Sadhguru Jaggi Vasudev, and her
journey toward self-enlightenment"--Provided by publisher.
    ISBN 978-1-57174-561-3 (5.25 x 7.25 tp : alk. paper)
    1. Simone, Cheryl, 1953- 2. Vasudev, Jaggi, Sadhguru. 3.
Spiritual biography. 4. Yoga. I. Vasudev, Jaggi, Sadhguru.
II. Title.
    BL1175.S4A35 2008
    295.4092--dc22

                                            2008001721

ISBN 978-1-57174-561-3
10 9 8 7 6 5 4 3
Printed on acid-free paper in Canada

TABLE OF CONTENTS

FOREWORD

Those of you who have read the phenomenal bestseller, *Eat, Pray, Love*, know of the many so-called pearls of wisdom "Richard from Texas" directed at the author, Elizabeth "Groceries" Gilbert. From the pages of her book, I gained, quite unexpectedly, some notoriety. The media dubbed me a "remarkable character that with his colloquial one-liners dispels poignant, irreverent, humorous advice." Others have gone so far as to characterize my persona as "so wise and possessing such an incredibly unique spirit." Even Oprah (that's *the* Oprah Winfrey) invited this "surprisingly wise cowboy" on her show that featured Liz and her runaway hit book.

Her readers also know of my former proclivities as a junkie and a drunk, along with my prior career as a drug dealer, or as Groceries more delicately labeled my line of work, a "commodities broker" in illegal narcotics. What you don't know is how the transformation occurred from that addict and alcoholic to a "Big Texas Yogi," who can emit what is alleged to be sage advice. Certainly the school of hard knocks taught me many lessons. But more importantly, I have been blessed with two remarkable teachers: first, the one Liz chose to keep anonymous (so I will too); and second, Sadhguru Jaggi Vasudev.

Even with my flourish and fanfare for memorable one-liners, I have no words that can even come close to describing this exceptionally incredible great being I am now graced to call my guru. I've never been in the presence of anyone like him before. He truly is one-of-a-kind. One could never label him what we preconceive in the U.S. to be a typical Eastern guru. He's very unorthodox, devoid of conformity, a jokester, frequently dons blue jeans and T-shirts, and loves to toss a Frisbee around. Yet, he epitomizes the very pinnacle of what a fervent seeker searches for in a spiritual guide—one who makes all possibilities available.

I first met Sadhguru in 2005 when a very dear friend, who had transformed so much herself, invited me to attend an introductory Inner Engineering Program. Well, to be truthful, she just didn't invite me—she bought my airline ticket and paid for the hotel and the class, so I couldn't say "no, I'm too busy, blah, blah, blah," or make some other excuse. So there I was sitting in the hotel meeting room and in walked this presence who actually made my body tingle. Then he turned and faced us.

I looked into his eyes and became dizzy. I was gazing into deep pools of love that just sucked me in and totally enveloped me. I had never had that kind of experience before. All I could think of was, "Oooohhhh, I'm in for some wild stuff." And then he opened his mouth and began to speak. When he talked, it resonated so deeply within me that I almost had a physical experience of his words. I felt that I was touched on a cellular level. To be more succinct, I was completely blown away.

At the end of the program, I spoke to him about my heart condition. You remember my prayer to open my heart that Liz wrote about? Resulting in a quadruple bypass? Well it was about five years later and problems had flared up again. I was eating nitroglycerin like it was candy, had suffered a heart attack, and was dodging the grim reaper. The doctors told me there was nothing more they could do and suggested that I get my affairs in order.

I asked Sadhguru if there was anything he could do to help me. He said, "Yes, but I don't have the time here, so you'll have to attend another specific program." The thought that ran through my mind was that he was a great salesman and had delivered a closing guaranteeing that I would come back.

So off I went to India for the next program, at the Wellness and Rejuvenation Center in his ashram adjacent to the foothills of the Vellingiri Mountains in Southern India. My treatment, individually designed by Sadhguru (as it was for all participants of the program), consisted of a combination of yogic practices, diet modifications, Ayurvedic therapies, and Siddha medicines. *Voila!* After a month I was living in a different body. My symptoms were no more. And the grim reaper—well, we put him to bed.

I now have attended every advanced course that Sadhguru offers, along with countless others. But what is unique is that, even though many attend a program, he mixes what he calls a "yogic cocktail" exclusively for each practitioner, blending all the aspects of yoga in just the right proportions, so everyone can achieve their longing. And I have. He has imparted an inner experience of esoteric Yogic teachings that have been around for thousands of years, but seemed totally out of reach for me. And all on a fast track, and I mean hold on to your hat.

The time I have spent around Sadhguru, practicing the methods he teaches, receiving the benefits of his myriad "technologies," and above all being showered with the Grace that flows so freely from him, is transformational. My life today is one of effortless living filled with joy, a deep sense of serenity, and freedom from many of the day-to-day entanglements. I feel so exceptionally fortunate and grateful to have this consummate gift of

Sadhguru in my life that I bestowed it upon my two sons, who now are on the path of Isha Yoga.

And now I wish to impart to you the same gift. This incredible being, Sadhguru Jaggi Vasudev, is available to you in *Midnights with the Mystic*. The book puts you in his presence in a very human way. It is written so that it is easy to grasp. You don't have to know anything about the subject matter to get what it teaches. But even seasoned readers will find fresh kernels of wisdom and understanding.

Cheryl Simone, the book's coauthor, had the great good fortune to have Sadhguru spend a week at her lake house so he could complete some needed work. During the evenings and into the night, she sat and conversed with him—such an amazingly rare experience for someone to be able to spend that kind of time with an enlightened being. So you, through the book, are invited to partake in that same incredibly rare experience.

You can take Cheryl's journey alongside her. You, too, can be the one sitting by the fire, riding in the boat, or gazing at the stars with Sadhguru, and all the while conversing with the world's greatest teacher—soaking in every aspect of his discernment. *Midnights with the Mystic* offers the unusual and insightful opportunity for you to share that personal space with this precious being and be a part of the metamorphosis that Cheryl underwent.

It is filled with all sorts of straightforward nuggets that are just plain useful. When you read this book, I know you'll resonate with its truths, be touched in ways that can trigger your own transformation, and realize, as I have, that a peaceful, fulfilling, and vibrant life is available for one and all who open themselves to receive the abundant Grace of this unparalleled being.

Midnights with the Mystic: Don't miss this rare opportunity. So sit back, relax, put your feet up, and get it straight from the horse's mouth.

—Richard Vogt, aka "Richard from Texas,"
a character in *Eat, Pray, Love* by Liz Gilbert

FOREWORD

As an independent editor and writer, I have had the good fortune to work with a number of wonderful and wise authors while writing on a variety of spiritual topics. When I read Cheryl Simone's manuscript about her experiences and Sadhguru Jaggi Vasudev, I felt an immediate kinship with the author. I also had a deep yearning to meet the unusual, fast-driving, humorous, and athletic guru she describes in her pages.

Some of Simone's experiences with Sadhguru are similar to experiences I have read in books about masters long dead. At the same time, Sadhguru seems to be so much more fun than the stereotype of the "hermit on the mountain." His sense of humor and his zest for life fairly leaped off the page. And, Simone's search for the right spiritual path to take her to a place of bliss sounds like my own decades-long hunt. This book, I realized, is about a journey into the heart of enlightenment.

Simone is the perfect guide into Sadhguru's world, especially for Westerners who may not have had much experience with gurus or enlightened beings. Simone asks the big questions. Her burning curiosity and sharp intellect help us probe into the depths of this pursuit. Some people might be understandably intimidated by so vigorous a man as Sadhguru, but Simone is absolutely clear on one thing: Sadhguru is the one person who can answer the questions that have been driving her for a lifetime, and she is not going to let the opportunity to find those answers pass her by. Although she had never written a book before, Simone's passion for her subject enabled her to convey her story in a straightforward and personable manner that helps make often abstract ideas accessible to anyone.

Simone initially approached the whole idea of a guru with a bit of old-fashioned skepticism. As she sheds her doubts, we cannot help but become convinced ourselves that Sadhguru is the real thing—a person who not only is able to dwell in the infinite, but who has the tools to help us go with him.

About eight months after I initially read the manuscript, I was able to take an Inner Engineering course with one of Sadhguru's teachers. Though Sadhguru himself was not there, his presence permeated the class, and some of the participants obviously had extraordinary experiences. The other thing I noticed was that all the volunteers who had been following Sadhguru's practices had a light shining in their eyes. I had never met people so kind and loving. They weren't pushy.

Well, I thought after this program, I'm obviously going to be a hard nut to crack. I did not have an awakening experience while in the course. I was my same old cranky self, but I was committed to my spiritual growth and I followed the prescribed practices. I also remembered Simone's rendering of her own spiritual tribulations. She tells us that she often wondered why other people seemed to have greater or deeper meditative experiences than she had, but she also reminds us that "experiences" are not the goal of this work—transformation is. And for some of us, it may take time to wear down our resistance.

Two weeks after taking the Inner Engineering course, I went to Sadhguru's *ashram* in Tennessee to take another program with the master himself. At first I simply thought I would enjoy myself; I had no hopes for feeling whatever it was other people seemed to feel. Two days into the program, my life was changed. In my journal I wrote: "I spent the weekend with a guru who slew my heart and turned my blood into furious rivers. I gasped for breath and plunged into those hungry waters. I wept in agony until I felt myself floating, held up by tiny goldfish.

On the shore, my broken shadow wailed and waved a dull sword. When it was time to go, I sailed away, my shadow trailing behind me. In the distance—drumming!"

I feel fortunate that I read this book prior to participating in the programs. I went in with an open mind and with an intellectual understanding of some of the concepts that we would discuss. I also realized that while it is a wondrously good thing to actually sit at the feet of the master and learn these techniques, it is the technology itself that can be life altering. Now that I have been following the practices that I learned in the programs, I have begun to experience the benefits that Simone described in her book: better health, more energy, greater focus, and moments of inexplicable joy.

For so long we've been told we need to live in the now. We've been told that "all this is an illusion" and that the "kingdom of heaven is within." Intellectually we may understand these ideas, but the difficult part for most of us seems to be how. How do we get from an intellectual understanding to a living experience? Thanks to Cheryl Simone and her book, I feel that I've taken a few baby steps on this path. I plan to advance much further, but even if I stayed here, I would have to say I'm much better off. A little bit of peace is a little bit of treasure.

For those meditators who have taken one or more of Sadhguru's programs, this book will provide answers to the questions you didn't even know you had. For others, such as myself, who had never even heard of Sadhguru before, reading this book will open your eyes and your mind to experiences you never imagined possible. It offers us great hope that we may not be limited to this merry-go-round of lifetimes. Enlightenment is possible. For us.

This is a book that must be read more than once. It is not simply a collection of pithy sayings; rather, it is an in-depth, involved conversation between a seeker and one who has found what the seeker is looking for. Each time you read it, you will understand it at a deeper level. Sadhguru's life story is in these pages. In fact, several of his life stories are here. His wisdom is also here. And even, I think, his love is here.

Namaste,

Pat MacEnulty

Author's Note: Pat MacEnulty has a PhD in creative writing from Florida State University. She is the recipient of several awards for screenplays and fiction writing. She is the author of four books, numerous short stories, essays, poems, and plays. Pat has also written several plays for young people, including *Puck and the*

Mushy Gushy Love Potion, which has been published by Heuer Publications. Currently, Pat is working on another novel and is adapting one of her books for film. She is also a teacher, workshop leader, writing coach, and freelance editor.

ACKNOWLEDGMENTS

My heartfelt gratitude to all of my friends and fellow travelers (both named and unnamed) who have touched this book in many different ways:

Sadhguru, who is beyond all that I can say. The many ways he has changed and expanded my life and is continuing to do so is the greatest of any and all gifts.

David Cochran, my co-creator in life and love, whose patience, support, and enthusiasm have helped me cross many speed bumps.

My son, who lovingly sacrificed spending time with me.

Swami Nisarga, sannyasin, who touched this book in many essential ways.

Rusty Fischer and Beth Bassett, editors, who helped turn an amazing experience into a book.

Pat MacEnulty, editor, whose assistance was invaluable and who is now on this journey with me.

Siobhan Donnelly, Gail Burns, Bobby, Swami Shailash, and Mike Snodgrass, whose enthusiasm, friendship, and tireless assistance in many different ways was priceless.

Ginger Price, New Leaf Distributing Company, who early recognized what we have here and was instrumental in helping to make it happen.

Raleigh Pinskey, who is a wonderful storehouse of PR knowledge and a pleasure to work with.

Bob Friedman and all of our other friends at Hampton Roads Publishing.

INTRODUCTION

There is a
Force within
That gives you life
Seek that
—Rumi

I met the mystic and self-realized Yogi Sadhguru Jaggi Vasudev after many years of fruitless searching. It was after I had hung up the search and vowed to live my life as best I could without the deep inner realization and serenity I sought that he came into my life and changed it.

In this man many people worldwide have seen someone beyond our imaginations. He is a being who is intensely alive in every possible way—in every human way and in every spiritual way. Whatever I had thought being human meant, he is more than that, and whatever I had imagined being a guru meant, he is also more than that.

Before I met Sadhguru, my quest for understanding took me to many different teachers on many different paths. I attended dozens of spiritual retreats, read many books on spirituality and philosophy, and traveled to spiritual places all over the world, including India, Nepal, Tibet, and Brazil. Still, after many years of trying, I hadn't gotten any closer to the answers I was seeking. I felt I'd actually come up empty-handed despite my considerable persistence and the intensity of my desire.

This is not to say that the paths I tried were not worthwhile; they just did not satisfy me. I did not have the confidence that they were going to take me where I wanted to go. So, after more than thirty years of searching that only resulted in disappointment, I was at a loss for what to do next.

Making this more frustrating and confusing was the fact that by "American dream" standards it looked as if I had really succeeded in life. I'd created a life abundant and rich in experiences and accumulation. I had love in my life, a wonderful family, plenty of friends, my own business, and lots of free time. I have a lake house in the mountains; I can go to the beach whenever I like. I have a loving and respectful partnership of twenty-six years, and even after all this time people say that he and I still light up when we see each other. My son and I are very close. You could say I have the whole package: great guy, wonderful son, cute dogs, and beautiful scenery.

And yet, there was no denying that I longed for something else. I ached for it—a bigger understanding, a bigger experience of life, a bigger indefinable *something*. People deal with this kind of dissatisfaction in many different ways, running the gamut from distraction to destruction. They drink, take drugs, have affairs, become obsessed with their work, or exercise like crazy. I tried to suffocate my own longing through comfort and keeping busy. Even though I knew in my gut that what I was looking for I would only find within myself, I kept hoping that some kind of fulfillment would come with the next accomplishment. Ultimately, the quest for success began to look like an endless series of goals, and I was getting bored chasing one goal after the other.

I not only got bored, I also felt guilty that even though I had everything I wanted, I was never completely satisfied. Was this really all there was to life?

In addition to having an undercurrent of restlessness and dissatisfaction, my abundant life had come at a cost: chronic stress, fatigue, hyperthyroidism, insomnia, and the accompanying prescription drugs.

I began asking myself, How is it that I could create a beautiful life for myself on the outside, yet inner peace, unconditional love, and self-knowledge remained so elusive? I've always been a positive, make-it-happen kind of person. I've never blamed God or the universe for anything in my life. But I began wondering if it was even possible for me to control my life and destiny in a much bigger way. Is it actually possible for an ordinary human to become completely free of ignorance and to gain inner realization, love, and self-mastery? Is permanent inner bliss possible for a person?

This book is the story of how I came to spend time with the Indian mystic and yoga master, Sadhguru, and how I discovered, in the course of exploring the subjects of life, death, and destiny with him, that real and lasting inner transformation was not only possible for me but was becoming a living reality. Several years after he initially came into my life, Sadhguru stayed with me for a week at my home in the mountains.

In this book, you'll join me on an extraordinary journey with him. While I have changed many of the names of the participants in this story, the words of Sadhguru and his amazing stories are truth in all meanings of the word. But first, we briefly travel the winding road that led me to him—or perhaps more accurately—that led him to me.

CHAPTER ONE
The Seeking: An American Story

I have climbed the highest mountains
I have run through the fields ...
I have run, I have crawled
I have scaled these city walls
Only to be with you
But I still haven't found
What I'm looking for.
—Bono/U2, 1987

From as early as I can remember, I have been a seeker. I did not know it at the time. I merely thought I was curious. As a child, I could not stand not knowing the answers to what I thought were the most basic questions: Where did we come from? Why are we here? How did a tree come out of a seed and a seed come out of the tree? How did something come out of nothing? Later the questions deepened. What happens after we die? Is there a God or a creator? What is the essential nature of my existence? I passionately wanted to unravel all life's secrets.

While religion and science offered explanations to most of the big questions, I was never comforted by these answers. I could never stifle that questioning voice that was longing to know more.

I was raised in Lexington, Massachusetts, a beautiful historic town with gorgeous colonial architecture and where the houses were set back off of the road on big, expansive, luscious, green lawns. It's an affluent town with affluent kids and a progressive, award-winning school system. My father was a successful entrepreneur and businessman; my mother was a homemaker. The Lexington schools were rated among the top in the state, which is one of the major reasons my father moved us there. If you did not want to send your kids away to private boarding schools, then you lived in Lexington. Many Harvard professors, scientists, engineers, and doctors live there. It is a picturesque historical New England town, nice and safe.

My first experience with death came when I was in first grade (prior to moving to Lexington, when we lived in Malden, Massachusetts). I remember that it happened one beautiful, warm, sunny day in the springtime and that the idyllic mood of a new beginning after the long winter was interrupted when the principal of the school came into our room. He gravely announced that a girl in my class had died and was never coming back. I didn't even know what "died" meant. I remember thinking, What does that mean, *she died?* Where could she have gone? How could she have just gotten sucked out of here like that? How could she possibly be gone forever? The questions ate at me. No one, including my parents (who were supposed to know everything), could answer these questions to my satisfaction.

Somehow, and I have no idea how since it was pretty far from where we lived and outside of the area I was allowed to explore (I was supposed to stay within the range of my mother's very embarrassing loud whistle), I found my way to the dead girl's house. It was a traditional two-story, New England-style, white, clapboard-siding house with black shutters on a large corner lot. I noticed a blue Schwinn girl's bicycle with a basket on the front leaning up against the house and I wondered if it was hers. Both of her parents were home, which surprised me because my dad would never have been home during the day. They were equally surprised to see me, but they welcomed me into the house. After a few minutes of conversation, they showed me into her bedroom. It's a strange feeling to go into the room of a dead person. Her room was painted white and had a pink bedspread and matching pink and white frilly curtains. I looked around at her toys, dolls, games, and stuffed animals neatly placed on the shelves. There were also several stuffed animals and dolls lying against the pillows on her bed. Her closet door was open as if she had just pulled out her dress for school.

As we stood there, I asked her parents every question I could think of. Surely they could offer me some answers about what had happened to her and where she had gone. They were her parents, after all. I don't even remember the specific questions I asked or how they responded. I do that remember they were kind to me and seemed happy to have me there. But the house felt like something huge was missing. It was as if there was a big black hole in it. When I tried to leave, I felt an invisible tug from her parents. They kept coming up with excuses for me to stay, offering me something to eat or drink and asking if I wanted to watch television. I felt so sad for them, but it was starting to get dark and I was about to be in big trouble if I didn't get home. I had not found any answers there, only enormous emptiness, loss, and grief.

The next time I encountered death I was ten years old. My grandfather died. My grandparents lived near us, and because my mission in life at the time was solely to have fun and adventures, I always snuck by or completely avoided their house as my grandfather always had an endless list of errands for me to do. Then he died. I felt terrible thinking about all the times I missed seeing him.

Even at ten, I remember thinking that I did not want to live my life in a way that I would be sorry for something I had or had not done. The temporary, ever-changing nature of things was beginning to sink in.

These experiences fueled and intensified my curiosity. I often wondered about death. It did not make me morbid or depressed; it just kept me curious and edgy.

As I aged, I read voraciously. I read philosophy, spirituality, religion, and anything that offered explanations about what happens when we die. Finding answers to life's questions also became entwined with wanting to know how to become more than just an ordinary person. Surely there was more to life than to be born, grow up, work, eat, sleep, make some money, and then die. In my readings, I found examples of people who were much more than the rest of us. I read about what Jesus, Buddha, and Confucius had to say. And I did not stop there. I also read about the occult, parapsychology, and witchcraft. I read anything that offered explanations beyond the scientific. I got extremely interested in what all the different masters from all the different traditions had to say. I wanted to know what they knew and how they came to know it. I wanted to know how they became masters. Were they born different from me?

All the living people I encountered when I was young, either through books or in person, were simply passing on what they had been taught or heard or read rather than what they had experienced for themselves. After many years of searching, I began to fear that I would die without knowing the truth. This was all the more frustrating because I had been told I had a good mind. In school I was placed in a program for gifted kids. It drove me nuts that I was supposed to be smart but that I still could not find the answers for myself.

At the same time, I harbored a slim hope that I would find my answers when I died. Maybe you have to die to know. But wait, I thought. Perhaps, and even worse, you could die and still not know. I kept wondering, Why can't I know while I am alive? Jesus and Buddha definitely seemed to know. And yet, they lived so long ago. It seemed everyone who knew anything was already dead— and they were not talking.

Then, strangely, when I was fifteen and home with the flu, a book just showed up on my front porch with a one-page note that read, "For Cheryl." I had never gone to the bookstore looking for that book; I didn't even know it existed. But, suddenly, *poof!* There it was, magically at my doorstep. I never did find out who left it there, but I am very happy they did.

This book was different from anything else I ever read. It was about yogis from the East and the path of yoga and where this yoga could take a person to reach their full human potential. This was totally new to me. I had encountered Hatha Yoga before, and it just looked like a series of stretching exercises that were supposed to be good for keeping your body flexible. This book, however, told about a mystic from India and how yoga had transformed him and some others into highly evolved, self-realized human beings. With the exception of the ancient masters like Buddha and Jesus, who were long ago deceased, I had never heard of anything like that before.

The book was *The Autobiography of a Yogi* by the Indian mystic Paramahansa Yogananda. Thanks to Yogananda, I found a name for the freedom I had been seeking: self-realization. Self-realization, which is also called enlightenment, was explained as the knowledge of one's true self beyond all illusion. It sounded as if we were all collectively suffering from a distorted view of reality in which we thought we were separate from everyone and everything else, when we were really all one energy. Einstein also said a few things that related to this concept. He said, "A human being is part of a whole, called by us universe, a part limited in time and space. He experiences himself, his thoughts, and feelings as something separated from the rest, a kind of optical delusion of his consciousness. This delusion is a kind of prison for us, restricting us to our personal desires and to affection for a few persons nearest to us. Our task must be to free ourselves from this prison. . . ." He also said, "Reality is merely an illusion, albeit a very persistent one."

According to Yogananda, we can come out of this illusion and know, understand, and experience life in a completely different way. It is described as a knowing that comes only through experience, rather than intellectual understanding, and it is felt in every cell of the body. Yogananda describes self-realization as the dissolution of the sense of a self as a separate ego personality into a blissful, ecstatic, boundless oneness that is free from death. Instantly I knew this is what I had been looking for!

Besides helping me to name the object of my quest, this book also gave me the hope that self-realization could be attained by ordinary people like me. It made me believe that I could actually and experientially know life outside of the prison of my small, separate identity. Yoga is a way to go from being limited to unlimited, the ultimate quest. What I was longing to know, I could know. I got so excited!

There was (of course) one major drawback. Yoga works best under the guidance of a guru. Yogananda glowingly describes a guru as a spiritual teacher who is a completely free being no longer bound by the illusion of a separate self, a being with access to other dimensions and a bigger understanding of life. A guru is said to be a dispeller of darkness and a remover of obstacles, someone able to help others out of the ignorance of their separate identities. I immediately thought that things would go much easier if I could be with such a spiritual teacher, and I wondered if I would ever find a guru.

Yogananda makes it clear that the most important thing that happened to him was that he had the incredible good fortune of finding his guru. As I read further, I got concerned. This relationship between a guru and a disciple did not sound like anything I was capable of. Yogananda's guru sounded very demanding. Self-realization and inner bliss was only found through discipline. Why is that, I wondered. What does discipline have to do with freedom?

Now I was in big trouble. This did not fit into my ideas at all.

I wanted the freedom and bliss, but at fifteen and as wild, adventurous, and undisciplined as I was, I didn't want to do the work or be told what to do. Besides that, the relationship sounded devotional, and that really made me squirm. I was definitely not into bowing down and worshipping another human being.

This was the 1960s, and did I mention that I was searching?

My quest for wisdom and fulfillment touched every area of my life. I spent my teen years in a roaring overdrive of experimentation and exploration. Lexington is a twenty-minute drive from Harvard University where, during that time, Timothy Leary and Richard Alpert (who later became Ram Dass), were professors and initiating

LSD experimentation. It was not long before LSD found its way into my safe high school. Lots of us began experimenting with it. One of my closest friends in those days, Barry, had a sister who attended Harvard, and she brought him some LSD to try. He tried it and loved it.

Although the nightly news delivered horror stories of people doing crazy things on LSD, Barry told me it would take me to new levels of understanding. So, I joined him in experimenting with the hallucinogen.

There was a big field not far from where I lived where a lot of kids from my school held parties. Our car stereos would blast Jimi Hendrix, Janis Joplin, and Jim Morrison. It was the perfect place to take an "acid trip." As soon as the LSD hit, I noticed that everything—the grass, the sky, the trees—seemed to be alive and teeming with a vibrant cosmic energy. Everything was living, loving, laughing, flying, crying, and dying all at the same time. What I considered to be me expanded and exploded to include the universe. It was incredible. Bliss without discipline. Excellent, I thought. I was convinced I was experiencing some of what Yogananda had described only without doing any of the work. What luck to have discovered this. A shortcut!

Until we crashed.

I had always sensed that there was a part of me that seemed to be observing my life as I lived it. During an LSD trip, I would experience that part of myself as if it were the "real" inner me. But, when the drug wore off, so did the experience. Each time my friends and I would expand into this much bigger consciousness and then have to return to this leaden reality. I could retain nothing, not any wisdom and definitely no permanent expansion or love from the experience. What it did leave me with was the frustration that there really was much more to life than what I normally experienced. Why was I only able to have a temporary glimpse of oneness, unconditional love, and bliss? This left me with a much deeper thirst and longing than before.

Back then, when so many people were trying to figure out the meaning of life, everything seemed so real and intense. For a minute we were invincible. We were going to change the world! Those were heady, restless, and reckless times full of a youthful longing to do something different and better. There was peace, love, great music, dancing, and protesting in the streets—such a wildly joyful time, so many people seemingly awake, living life full-tilt, *on* all the time.

But, at the same time, people were dying all around us.

As we stuck daisies in the soldiers' rifles to protest for peace, the TV showed other soldiers coming home in caskets. We saw firsthand the casualties of Vietnam on both sides. We watched history being made. And we were appalled. At home, our friends were dying of drug overdoses both accidental and on purpose. Young, vital people died in car and motorcycle accidents going so fast, literally and figuratively, taking crazy chances, thinking they could never die. It was all such a terrible waste.

Barry was very smart and always had to be learning something. His father was a Harvard professor. Barry was the only person I knew who would just pick up the encyclopedia and read it for fun. Every subject seemed to interest him. There was also a very reckless side to him, and I often wondered what was going to become of him.

One time he and another friend named Mike, who were purported to have the highest IQs of anyone in the school, were having an argument about who was the smarter one. They were supposed to be within one or two IQ points of each other, and in that geeky group, they thought that was some sort of a big deal. They both turned to me and asked me who was the smarter. I had known Mike for years, but Barry, being my boyfriend, smugly figured that I would side with him.

I shocked him by saying, "Mike's definitely smarter than you are, Barry."

Barry, in disbelief, said, "What! How can you say that? You really know me. You *know* how smart I am. If anyone knows how smart I am, you do."

"Yes," I answered, "and that's why I know without question that Mike is smarter than you. Mike is going to make something of himself, and what I know about you is that you are most likely going to crash and burn."

Barry and I stayed friends after we later split up, often talking on the phone, and he wrote to me when I was at college. But I later kept a distance from him. I no longer wanted anything to do with drugs. I knew that if I did not change my life, I was going to self-destruct.

I don't know what happened to Mike, but Barry was found dead of a drug overdose when he was twenty-five. His sister had committed suicide a few years earlier. When I heard the news of Barry's sister I felt sick to my stomach. I was so sorry for her and very concerned about how this was going to affect Barry. When Barry died, I just wished I or someone could have done something. I had so hoped he was going to pull himself out of the path he was on. The drugs that had started out as fun turned deadly. Both of them had seemingly perfect, gifted lives and wasted them at such young ages. My heart just broke for their parents losing two of their children. It was inconceivable to me how they could bear such a tragic and unnecessary loss. By the time Barry died, I was already a mother of a three-year-old and I could not imagine how Barry's mother was going to survive losing her children.

These experiences with death in my youth, starting with the little girl in grade school, who I didn't really know at that time, and then extending out into my circle of friends, fueled my quest for understanding and caused me to never deny or pretend that death would not eventually overtake me and everyone I loved. The magnitude and inevitability of death was often in my thoughts and kept my searching alive.

As a generation we had no one, really, to guide us. We did not trust anyone who was part of the establishment or even over the age of thirty. I think that the same youthful energy that was so scattered and uncontrolled back then could have led to deep and lasting transformation, both within us and in the world, if we had the right leadership and guidance to help channel that energy in a constructive way.

Right before I read *Autobiography of a Yogi*, I also became interested in meditation, as incompatible as this seems with all the wildness of my life back then. I was not looking at meditation as a discipline; I was looking at it as fun. At the age of fifteen, I started my formal study of meditation and mind control with a spiritual teacher named Margie, who was somewhat of a local celebrity in the Boston area, giving spirituality talks on the radio. I met Margie through my father. She and the wife of one of his business associates taught a meditation/mind control class.

Margie was about forty-five years old and had been a devout Catholic for years. About ten years before I met her, she had become disillusioned with the church and began to study with many different teachers from different traditions. She was smart, serene, and lots of fun. Even though she was much older and wiser, she also seemed to stay part teenager. There was something about her that made everyone who came into contact with her feel good. She lived in Concord, Massachusetts on a five-acre estate. Her house was a cute, little, yellow former-caretaker's cottage set in a wooded area quite a distance from the main house. To me, the place was enchanting, and in my young mind knowing Margie was like having a fairy godmother. She was interested in all the Eastern religions as well as in parapsychology, mind control, and the development of psychic abilities. It was clear after spending time with her that she was somewhat clairvoyant. She sometimes seemed to know things before I told her, often answering the phone with the answer to a question or comment I had not yet asked. It was really amazing. No one else I knew was like that and before I met her, I did not believe any such thing was possible.

One time she and I were planning on going to the ballet, but a friend showed up at my house from out of state. He had traveled all day just to surprise me and was only going to be in town for that one evening. I told him that, unfortunately, I already had plans for that night and if I could not reach Margie to cancel, I would not be able to go anywhere with him.

I tried to call Margie three times in a row, and at the end of the third call, with my finger on the button and the receiver still in my hand I told him I was sorry; I had to go to the ballet. At that very moment, the phone rang. It was Margie. Her first words were, "Sorry I wasn't at home to get your call. I don't want to go either." It shocked us! This kind of stuff often happened with her, though, and after a while it seemed normal.

Margie also taught me about reincarnation, which fascinated me. I had only heard of it before in the primitive context presented in my elementary school, and I thought it had something to do with being reborn as a cow or some other animal. Margie gave me a couple of books to read about reincarnation. What I read and what Margie said made much more sense than the other explanations of what happens after death that I'd heard up until then. She said this life was a progression and that a human birth was a big opportunity to know your original god nature. This fascinated me. But again, while reincarnation satisfied my curiosity more than other explanations, it remained theoretical as I obviously had no experiences to back it up.

This wonderful teacher was not only instrumental in introducing me to the study of meditation; she also introduced me to my first husband, Ted, when I was seventeen.

Margie taught a meditation class in the local prison, where Ted was one of her students. He was in jail for manslaughter. At age sixteen, he'd had a fight with a boy who tragically died as a result. Margie adored Ted. She talked about how wise and kind he was, and she wanted me to meet him.

Are you kidding? I thought. Why would I want to meet him? The last thing I wanted to do was to meet anyone in a prison, and I also did not want Margie "fixing me up" with anyone—even though she denied that it had anything to do with that.

She kept talking about him, however, and occasionally she would bring me to the prison with her. Eventually, I met him.

Ted was nineteen when we met, and soon to be eligible for parole. Despite the fact that Ted was incarcerated, he lived like a yogi. He had his own cell and spent most of his time reading, meditating, fasting, and doing yoga. He was quite shining and beautiful at the time, and he seemed much deeper than anyone I'd ever met—with perhaps the exception of Margie. His spiritual thirst was so strong that my own spiritual thirst very naturally bonded with his. Not one of the other boys I knew had any interest in spirituality. We fell in love and planned to be together as soon as it was possible. It seemed that I was headed into bliss after all.

When he was granted his parole, we immediately planned to get married. I was nineteen. I was fully conscious of what a terrible decision this looked like on my part and of all the consequences of such a decision, but I felt strongly that if my spiritual thirst was genuine, I had to go in that direction. My father had moved us to Lexington to ensure that I would have the best education possible and all the "right opportunities." Even though many of the girls I grew up with blatantly spoke of money, success, and status, and marrying "right," I had no such intentions. I was not really interested in marriage, a big wedding, or any of the trimmings. I was only interested in love. I was flying high and knew in my heart that Ted and I would last forever in our spiritual bliss.

However, my engagement drove a huge wedge between my family and me, and especially between my father and me. My father had endless discussions with me about what an enormous mistake I was about to make. Once he finally realized that no matter what he did or said he could not change my mind or control my actions, he got so exasperated that he not only refused to attend the wedding, he also quit speaking to me. He made it abundantly clear that he did not want to have anything to do with me. For a time, I was dead to him.

This was a huge loss to me because I was crazy about my father, and I knew that he adored me. Until then he had always been my biggest fan and supported everything I did. He was very hard-working. He would often leave for work before dawn and not return until after dark, yet he was attentive enough of me to notice what I was up to and that I was reading all sorts of things that were out of the mainstream, things about meditation and spirituality. That's the reason he told me about Margie's meditation class. In fact, when I said I'd take the class if he would, he agreed and we took it together. He not only introduced me to my first spiritual teacher, he shared in the experience with me. Rather than frown on it as something weird, he was willing to take the time to explore it with me.

I hoped that, in time, my father would soften toward me and eventually get to know Ted (which he eventually did). I knew he was only concerned about my well-being and he was doing all he could do to influence me. Even though I knew this, it weighed heavily on me because the last thing I wanted to do was cause my father any suffering.

As for me, I did not care about Ted's past. I cared only about who he was when I met him. Spiritual growth was more important to me than anything else in my life, and I thought this relationship was meant to be. I thought we would be on a spiritual path together. I knew

I had found my soul-mate. For a time, I continued to believe this.

But things change. We moved to the Midwest, where Ted was paroled and where his parents lived. Ted found a job doing skilled machine work. The hours were long, and the town where we lived was dreary and cold. I was away from friends and family, but Ted and I were very close, so I was happy even though I did not like where we lived. A year later I found a job for him with friends of mine in sunny Florida. Ted was able to get his parole transferred, so we moved. I really wanted us to live somewhere beautiful and warm.

Ted had somehow managed to create a spiritual cocoon of sorts for himself inside a very harsh environment when he was in prison and had a lot of time to work on himself. But when he got out, the distractions of being outside in the real world and trying to earn a living created new challenges for him. He was extremely responsible and was obviously capable of great discipline, but with working twelve to fourteen hour days, the meditation, fasting, and yoga he had been doing became a thing of the past. The radiance, peace of mind, and sense of humor that had been present in him before was no longer as accessible.

Ted was also a talented musician with an amazing voice. Music seemed to easily transport him to his easy-going self, but his overall day-to-day life was not lived with a sense of ease.

What I didn't appreciate fully at the time was how traumatic it is to spend four years in prison. It takes time for people to recover. I was wide open, an open book; Ted was a much more private person, which often put us at odds. We were very different from each other, much more different than I realized. Somehow, probably because of the whole soul-mate fantasy, I expected us to experience things the same way. The way I was made Ted uncomfortable, and the way he was left me feeling suffocated. Things became so uneasy between us that we could not even do something simple together, like go to a movie, and have it go smoothly. Little by little we lost our intimacy and our sense of fun. We became just another mundane, at odds, unhappy couple. I was heartbroken about what was happening to us, but I still hoped we could fix it. What had been beautiful, thrilling, and miraculous such a short time earlier completely unraveled. Like every other "high" I had experienced in my life, this one also left.

Then at twenty-two, I gave birth to my son, Chris. Ted and I were both so ecstatic about Chris. We were flying! The bliss was back! I barely slept for weeks. It was such a miracle, nothing could bring us down. For a time it seemed to mask the difficulties we were having in the marriage. About a year later, Ted had some opportunities to do something with his music and we moved to Atlanta.

Shortly after we moved, like a tape on fast forward, the marriage came to a crashing halt. Out of what I thought was the blue, Ted asked for a divorce. I should have seen it coming, but not that many people divorced back then. It was like being hit in the stomach. It took my breath away. I had no idea that once we were married and had a child, changing our minds was an option. I thought we had married for life and that the marriage, though rocky, was something we would work on. When I look at it now, I know that neither one of us was happy in the relationship, but it just never occurred to me that it would not become good again. At that point, I was totally involved and focused on being a good mother. My concern about the marriage had taken a backseat.

I did not realize it at the time, but I don't quit things. I now have had the same business partner (who is also my very good friend) for twenty-one years, my lawyer for eighteen years, and (though we're not officially married) my second husband for more than twenty-five years. Although this can be a good characteristic, it is not always the right decision. Sometimes, like the song says, you have to "know when to fold 'em."

For the next couple of years, I would not let go and we struggled with the relationship. The deep passion was gone for both of us, but I still wanted to keep the marriage together. Ted, on the other hand, felt he had already missed the prime of his life in prison, and now he was not happy in the marriage. He said he did not want to "waste" any more of his life. Ouch!

This was not supposed to happen, I thought. This was a relationship that was meant to be. After that, I became quite cynical about relationships. I no longer believed in some juvenile idealistic idea of soul-mates or that anything was "destined to be." Again, the ever-changing, impermanent nature of life had left its mark on me.

Getting divorced felt like getting ripped to shreds. I had never before experienced such a personal loss. The other losses in my life had certainly shaken me, but this was deeper and much more personal. It made me understand in a very real way how all things eventually end. Even if your marriage works out well, it doesn't go on forever. The phrase "till death do us part" points out the inevitable. Later, when I found love again, I didn't blow it out of proportion and burden it with soul-mate status. With anything that's impermanent, and relationships are a prime example, whatever happens, however good or bad, someday it's over.

So, what is it that's never over? Is there something in us that does not die? Love wasn't it, even though I thought love was the best that life had to offer.

Yogananda says that you die a thousand deaths until you're liberated. Whatever this liberation is, I wanted it.

My pride was so bruised by the failure of my marriage that an entire year went by before I told my parents about it. When my mother would call and ask, "So how's Ted?" I would say, "He's fine" as if nothing had changed. Ted and I were maintaining a friendship of sorts. I knew that he was fine, so I wasn't lying.

I was in no hurry to break the news to my parents. No one in my family had ever divorced, and I felt a huge amount of embarrassment over the failure of my marriage, particularly because of the stand I'd made. Practically everyone who mattered to me, including all my friends (except Margie), had opposed the marriage. Even Barry tried to talk me out of it and said it would not be like I was imagining it to be and that Ted would be different than I expected. The way I saw it, the divorce was the biggest failure of my life.

Even though they could easily have helped me, I embarked on this next phase of my life without asking my parents for any help at all. They lived in another state and I only spoke to them once a week. I would never admit to them that I was having a hard time. That part of my life was over, and for better or worse, my survival and my son's survival was up to me.

Although I was in tremendous pain from losing not only the love of my life but also my sense of security, I did not want to talk about it. I hated to be vulnerable. I did not want to discuss it at all until I had my sense of balance back. I was a problem-solver, a fixer; I wasn't normally emotional, but this time my emotions had me completely hijacked. At some point I think I bought into the idea that emotions were weakness. I did not believe in whining or complaining about life when it is going wrong; you just do the best you can to fix things and move on. I mainly looked at life's challenges as speed bumps, but this situation was huge to me.

On the radio Helen Reddy was singing, "I am woman, hear me roar." But roaring was not happening for me. I was a single parent, broke, and in way over my head. I was not only completely on my own, I was also totally clueless about how to be a good mother and how to make money—let alone do them both at the same time! But, I did have my pride.

When I was young and my parents were supporting me, I looked around and saw that even people with money did not seem to be happy, so I thought that money was not important or—at least very overrated. I did not know how young, immature, and even arrogant that thinking was and how easy it is to think this way when someone else is taking care of all your monetary needs (particularly in quite a beautiful style). I still know that money and happiness are unrelated, but the level of suffering created when the basics of life aren't covered . . .

this was something I had no idea about. I realized just how important money was to me once I didn't have any. I had never before experienced the fear of not having enough money; never before had I been gripped with fear about anything—it can be practically paralyzing.

Ted paid his child support, but it barely made a dent in our expenses. Being responsible for providing food and shelter for me and a baby overwhelmed me. When I was married, Ted handled it. I worked some, but whether I did or not did not really matter to him. Like my father, Ted took on the responsibility for making money. I had no career path, no training of any sort, and really had never had to work before. I had gone to college on and off, but I never sought a degree. I took enough courses to graduate, but I never found a field I was interested in. There was nothing I wanted to be. I started in philosophy, but they had the same questions I had, and as far as I was concerned, no answers. I thought I was interested in psychology, but they did not seem to have answers either. So, I just took courses I was interested in, such as Eastern religions and English, without any specific goals. Now I was faced with many of the bad decisions I'd made, like not choosing a career path. What kind of job could I get? Again, it turned out that I was not so smart after all. I was determined to be independent, but I was also really worried.

In many ways, I thought my life was finished. I was only twenty-five, but things had begun to look hopeless.

My friends were doing all kinds of fun and interesting things. They were traveling the world. They were sky diving, scuba diving in the tropics, skiing in Switzerland, taking cooking classes in Paris. They were traveling to Europe, India, and Egypt. I was working two jobs: one that did not pay me anything and one I did not particularly like. And, as if this were not enough, I was living in constant fear of not having enough money and of growing old alone.

I sank into what we'd now call a clinical depression. I woke up depressed, went to sleep depressed, and felt depressed throughout the day. I couldn't shake it. It was as if I were enveloped in a thick, heavy fog that possessed me. It suffocated me. The depression was like a living entity. It wanted to live, to suck out all my life energy. I quite simply had no hope for the future. I'd never experienced anything like this. I'd been a happy and fun-loving pleasure seeker, and now my life was devoid of anything resembling happiness.

It took me a full year to climb out of this all-consuming depression and become happy again. Once I had fallen that deep, it was very difficult to climb out. When I did find my way out, I took my state of mind very seriously. I knew I would never go back there. I would never allow myself to sink into a state like that again. It was crystal clear to me that my happiness was my sole responsibility. I did not need anyone else to make me happy; it was within me and me alone. I was very careful after that where I would allow my thinking to take me and what I would allow my thoughts to land on. I also very strongly felt that I never wanted to get married again. I did not trust my judgment about men and did not want any more children. Since I was happy again, I felt no need to be in a relationship.

The first job I took was as an apartment manager at the complex where I lived, which only gave me a free apartment and barely enough money for food and gasoline. It turned out that I was very good at getting the apartments rented, so the owners started sending me to their other properties that were not renting very well. Someone I knew said, "Cheryl, you are so good at this! You would be great in real estate and you would make a lot more money."

I liked getting the apartments leased. It was fun to make something happen. The idea of doing something I enjoyed and making more money at the same time sounded great. I looked into it and decided that becoming a realtor was a good idea for me.

I took a job as a cocktail waitress so I could go to real estate school during the day. I was really ready to make some decent money. I did not want not having enough money to be an issue in my life. All I could think about was getting my license so I could solve my money problems and get back to the lifestyle I was more comfortable with, one that I had so recklessly thrown away. However, once I did get my real estate license, I was worse off. I no longer had a guaranteed paycheck. When I did make a sale, it could be weeks or months before it closed. If we had a crisis, such as a tire blowout or anything out of the ordinary, I didn't have the money for it. One time I had a bad case of the flu and missed a week of work. I couldn't pay the electric bill and had to borrow money from a friend to keep the power on. I had never before experienced how something you take so easily for granted could completely dislocate your life.

I also had no idea how difficult it is to take care of a baby. The demands of providing for the two of us meant I was away from him more than either one of us wanted. Chris would often get mad at me because he didn't like me being gone. One time, when he was only four years old, he banged his little fist on the dinner table and exclaimed, "When I go to my friend's house, his mother is there. She is always there! Where are you?" I was a working, single mother. What could I say to make him understand?

Sometime during all this, good things were also happening. I met David, my current but unofficial husband, and fell head over heels in love again, in spite of my cynicism about the whole love thing. It is still, to this day, one of the best things that ever happened to me. Being in love is great fun. The initial high is hugely blissful. You feel in love with the world. The initial drug-like euphoria, while wonderful, always settles down. To have a wonderful friend and companion that you adore is a huge gift of life that I have been fortunate enough to experience for many years.

I soon gave up the waitress job and took on a paper route with the newly formed newspaper called *USA Today* because it made pursuing real estate easier. My job was to deliver papers into the newspaper boxes around town, and it paid fairly well. I could be finished working in about two hours, even before most people woke up in the morning. This required taking Chris with me on the route since it started at four in the morning. The only time I had seen that hour of the morning before was when I stayed up for it. Staying up for it was much easier and fun than getting up at that hour. I hated that alarm clock.

One day when we were out delivering papers, a guy in a beat-up car started to follow us. Concerned, I tried to figure out what to do. Where was the closest police station? Where could we go where people would be around? Chris popped awake. He saw the car and the guy, and he looked at me. He looked again at the car and he looked back at me and said, "If somebody wanted to hurt us, is there anything at all that you could do about it?"

I was having the same thought! We got lucky and a cute, young policeman came to our rescue.

Even though this particular incident turned out all right, the responsibility of trying to keep my child safe and all the emotions accompanying that responsibility I felt at a magnitude that I could never have imagined before becoming a mother.

Shortly after I got my real estate license, I informed my friends that in three years, when I was eligible to be a broker, I would have my own real estate company. This was a pretty bold claim since I was struggling just to make enough money keep me and Chris clothed, fed, and comfortable as we lived from commission to commission.

Soon after I made this statement, a loan officer discovered me and started introducing me to his builder clients. Suddenly I had more work than I could handle and the money flowed in! I liked the work and put a lot of time and energy into it. Three years after I had my real estate license, to the month, someone else introduced me to some investors, and I started my own business.

Approximately two years later, with the help of my current business partner, I bought out the guy who was my first money partner. I later got into house building and land development as well. For the most part, I have lived a very affluent life; but one thing about real estate is that it is market-driven and a little bit like gambling in Las Vegas. You can make a lot of money, but if the economy goes south or you make some bad decisions, you can also lose a lot of money. Even though things have gone very well for many years, it has never seemed absolutely stable, and I was often stressed out about my business.

While making money and growing my career, I also went after my inner growth. I moved along these two avenues simultaneously: the business, self-help, personal growth arena, and the spiritual arena. By now, I was actually more comfortable in the business field. I didn't see my growth as a business person as separate from the process of finding spiritual freedom. It was something I could apply and see the results of. Even the business book authors, such as Tony Robbins and Napoleon Hill, often pointed to something much bigger, something untapped inside of us.

I also explored different types of yoga. I started with the lessons offered from Yogananda's foundation through the mail (which I sent off for shortly after I read his book).

Over the years, I found a wide variety of other living teachers as I took part in many classes and retreats. In addition to yoga, I tried a variety of other things: Transcendental meditation, Zen meditation, Vippasaana meditation, and Tibetan Buddhism. Each of these paths had their own success stories about individuals who had found enlightenment, or at least transformation, through their practices.

Each practice interested me at first, but despite several years of involvement with these various paths, they left me feeling hopeless. For some reason, I did not particularly like the practices and I was not able to trust that they would really work for me. Small things were happening, but it just seemed to me that even if I dedicated my entire life to one or more of them, it would take an eternity for something substantial to happen. I am extremely results-oriented, and even with a sufficient amount of time spent on the various methods, I could not see much or enough transformation in myself. This is not to say that the paths I tried weren't worthwhile; they just did not seem to be "it" for me.

I knew that my expectations were extremely high. I wanted enlightenment. Maybe my expectations were actually the problem, but it was impossible for me to set them aside. After all, Yogananda's book had convinced me that reaching the peak was possible, and I couldn't rest until I climbed to the top. His book had made it sound like yoga was a very quick, direct path to enlightenment, so I never lost interest in yoga.

Even though I was disappointed with my progress so far, my various studies were not a waste. Thanks to the many spiritual disciplines I practiced over the years, I did find some measure of freedom. Emotionally, I stayed steady and for the most part pretty upbeat. I learned to create a little more space between my thoughts and actions—actually between my feelings and reactions. This is extremely important; without it, life can be a real roller coaster ride.

Along the way I also met a variety of interesting and beautiful people. I met the Dalai Lama and even hosted a high Tibetan Rinpoche and his attendant, who lived with my husband, son, and me for eight months. Rezong Rinpoche is highly revered in the Tibetan community. He spent nine years in silence while living in a cave during this lifetime. His inner light and depth of understanding truly shines brightly from within him. When he spoke at a class about "emptiness being quite full, actually," I felt that he was speaking from his own experience.

The entire time the Buddhists stayed with us, they meditated and chanted daily—all day and late into the evening. I would often wake up at three or four o'clock in the morning and hear them chanting.

Although their lives were full of spiritual discipline, they were not overly serious, and there was constant laughter. The atmosphere of our home changed while they were there. It felt charged somehow. Although I loved having their company, and knowing them enriched my journey, their paths did not resonate with me as a way to transform myself.

Other teachers I encountered included Swami Muktananda and Ram Dass. I went to see Swami Muktananda in college with several of my friends. We had heard that he was an enlightened being and that people often had spontaneous experiences of their inner *kundalini* responding to the spiritual master in a way that caused them to chant, dance, or perform yogic hand movements that were previously unknown to them. My friends and I, ever the skeptics, talked about that on the way to see the Swami. We decided that unless something like that happened to one of us, we would keep our doubts intact. Swami Muktananda was a glowing being, and many people did seem to respond unusually to him. They danced and sang, and were visibly moved by the Swami, but for some reason, I did not feel any connection to him. I was turned off to the entire scene I found there, the frenetic movement and the crying. It was not for me.

In spite of my thirst for spirituality, I have always been extremely averse to all spiritual scenes where people seem to lose control. I also still harbored a lot of judgment about "masters" or "gurus." In my immaturity, I really thought devotion was for stupid people who were looking for someone to tell them what to do. Not only was I bothered by spiritual scenes, a part of me was also pretty mainstream. I was more comfortable with business people and intellectuals than with spiritual seekers and people in the New Age community. I definitely did not want to be involved in anything that looked like a cult.

I also met the American spiritual teacher Ram Dass and went to many of his talks and retreats. Ram Dass was easy for me to relate to. He was an intellectual and spoke in terms I could understand. Like me, Ram Dass had experimented with LSD. During an early meeting with Ram Dass, I had a profound mystical experience (which I will talk about later) that I could not explain. Because of that particular experience, I asked him if he was my guru. I was not necessarily looking for a guru, but I thought perhaps my guru might have found me. But Ram Dass said no, he was in no way a guru. He said that when I met my real guru, I would know it. He had spent a few years in India with his guru, Neem Karoli Baba. He told me that sometimes when someone's seeking is intense, things will happen through him. I came away feeling disappointed. Yet, at the same time, I had even more confidence that somehow my own inner self would guide me to freedom.

Over time, I also met several other people who were said to be enlightened. Some of the people who did appear to me to have a bright inner light shining from within had spent time around someone purported to be enlightened. In other words, like Ram Dass, they had had a living guru.

I started to think that in order to experience real life-changing inner transformation, I needed to be around an enlightened, self-realized being—if there really was such a being.

Even though I considered my life to be happy and on some levels complete, I continued to have a certain deep, disappointed wariness. Is this really all there is to life? I wondered.

I knew that what I wanted the most, I still didn't have. But me, have a guru? Was it really a guru I was looking for?

Intellectually, I knew that even with some measure of worldly success, I still had no mastery over spiritual things. There was no denying that after thirty years.

What's ironic is that I've never hesitated to consult with or ask an expert for guidance in my business. But with experts, you're working with them on your own terms. I had no idea what it meant to have a guru; you're getting into a realm where you're not sure if it's going to be on your terms or not. First of all, would I even be able to recognize a true guru? Second, what if I am not capable and unable to do what is needed?

What I didn't know then is that when you're truly sincere and ready for help, you develop a certain receptivity. You become willing to set aside your doubts and concerns and take a leap into the unknown.

Finally, one day I broke down, set aside my pride, and asked the universe—or the infinite or whatever I was calling "it" at the time—for help. I have never been comfortable asking for any kind of help, so this was not a casual request. It had come only after a long struggle to find the object of my quest on my own. I concluded that without some sort of extraordinary help, nothing of a truly deep and transformational nature was ever going to happen to me. Faster than I could imagine the end of my life would arrive, and this ephemeral gig would be up, once and for all with or without the answers I had searched for so many years.

So, I gave up.

It was not a big event. No lightning in the sky or thunderbolts followed my humble request for help. But something seemed to have clicked. Afterward, an unfamiliar peace descended upon me. Although nothing had changed on the outside, a certain serenity entered me. Somehow I felt that my journey was seriously underway at last.

Within months, I found myself placed in front of a person who would prove to be as mystical as he was simple.

CHAPTER TWO
The Finding: Encountering Sadhguru

"This life for me is an endeavor to help people experience and express their divinity. May you know the bliss of the divine."
—Sadhguru

One day not long ago, an exuberant man from South India was traveling in the country north of Vancouver, Canada. Seeing that his car needed gasoline, he stopped at the first station he came to, a rural one deep in the Canadian woods. He had just gotten out of his car and begun to fill his tank when he noticed an old Native American man leaning against a nearby pick-up truck and looking at him intently. The two men did not know each other, but soon the older man slowly walked toward the man pumping gas.

When he was near, he said to the man from India, "The winds told us of your coming, brother," and he bowed respectfully.

The mysterious and poetic words of the old Native American are not a surprise to those of us who have gotten to know Sadhguru. To us, he seems at once to be very much a part of the day-to-day rhythms of life and yet so completely beyond them; it's not surprising that even the wind would sing with news of his coming to those who are listening. I heard the story of Sadhguru's encounter with the old Native American from my friend and his assistant, Leela, long after the events I am writing about here.

Unlike the old man, I first heard about Sadhguru in an entirely mundane way.

I was sitting at a gate in the Phoenix airport waiting for my connecting flight to arrive on my way to a silent retreat being held in Santa Barbara, California when I noticed a young man sitting in peaceful meditation, oblivious to the hustle that surrounded him. Since I rarely see people meditating (especially in airports) and since I was heading for a meditation retreat myself, he stood out to me. Coincidently, on the leg back from

California, much to my surprise, this same young man came and sat down next to me at the airport while I was again waiting to board my plane. We soon struck up a conversation. Since I instantly remembered him as the man I saw meditating earlier, I asked him about it. He told me that he had been interested in meditation for years. That led to me talking about my meditation experience at the retreat I had just been on. His meditation looked like it was working; mine wasn't.

Unfortunately, my experience with solitude this time had not been particularly good. Even after spending an entire week in silence I had not come away with any feeling of peace. On the contrary, I felt more agitated than when I arrived. I was even more painfully aware of all I failed to understand and of all the attachments and fears I had accumulated over the years. I felt as if I was suffocating. Peace of mind did not seem remotely possible for me. We were not very far into a conversation when he told me about his guru, Sadhguru.

Sadhguru sounded interesting to me, even intriguing. I wondered why I had not heard of Sadhguru before. As the young man repeated some things this guru had said, I became sufficiently interested in knowing more. What really struck me, however, was not the young man's enthusiasm, but how much he felt that he had changed since meeting Sadhguru.

"Since meeting Sadhguru and practicing the yoga that he transmits and teaches, I have dropped many of the fears and attachments that have dogged my life since childhood," he said. He went on to tell me that he had periodically suffered from panic attacks since childhood in addition to feeling loads of stress and anxiety. He also claimed that he suffered with chronic insomnia. You would never know it to sit with him. He was so calm and centered; he looked like an advertisement for yoga and meditation. I sat there thinking that I still must not know how to meditate because it was not working even after all this time and effort. When I voiced that thought to him, he told me that prior to meeting Sadhguru the same had been true for him, even though he also had meditated for years.

I was not used to hearing such glowing accounts of lasting benefits. Sure, small changes are common to people when they first meet a teacher or discover a new retreat, book, or philosophy. But, he claimed that only after meeting Sadhguru and learning the practices that Sadhguru had taught him that he underwent a significant life transformation. I wondered if it was possible that this young man had actually found an authentic, living guru. Something seemed to be working. He definitely had an unusually pleasant and peaceful demeanor.

But my skeptical side would not be so easily per-suaded. To begin with, there was way too much reverence in his description of Sadhguru to suit me, and this left me cold. There's nothing like an overabundance of devotion to rankle me. On top of that, he said that Sadhguru had an organization of more than five hundred thousand volunteers worldwide, which made me uncomfortable just hearing about it. I personally have never liked groups. With the exception of a few professional organizations, I have always avoided joining anything. I particularly disliked "spiritual scenes." I even wondered if this had the flavor of a cult.

He also mentioned various altered states of energy that happened to people around Sadhguru. He went so far as to say that Sadhguru often left people drunk and ecstatic for many days and that sometimes people have to be carried out of the meditation hall. This really sounded farfetched. In my travels over the years I had seen some unusual things, but I had never encountered anything quite like that, so my agnostic radar became fully engaged. Through the Tibetans I had met though, and because I was an avid reader, I had heard of many stories that sounded a bit far out about people behaving strangely around so-called masters. And, I had seen for myself people behaving very unusually around Swami Muktananda, but this sounded a bit much. Since I had personally never experienced any such thing, I was doubtful as to the genuineness of the behavior.

Besides, there have been many accounts of exceptional teachers from the East who have ended up being a disappointment to many people, and they have caused gurus in general to have a bad standing in this country. We've all heard in the media about the few who've made spirituality into either a big business or who have created scandals of one sort or another.

Yet in spite of my skepticism, I was definitely curious since I had just ended yet another spiritual retreat without feeling like I was doing anything with myself. Still, I could not help but venture a question, "So how many limousines does Sadhguru own?"

The young man was speechless. He looked stunned and disappointed. In the awkwardness of the moment, I felt a bit embarrassed at my insensitivity. He quickly recovered and suggested I check out Sadhguru for myself.

On the basis of this one conversation, I figured that Sadhguru must be a truly charismatic person, even though my inner skeptic considered it highly unlikely that he was an enlightened being. After all this time, part of me doubted if there really was such a thing as enlightenment.

As I said, I was very discouraged to have ended another spiritual retreat without making any progress, and it was continuously and painfully obvious to me that despite my effort and perseverance, I was not getting anywhere close to where I wanted to be. When I could get past my own pride, I knew I wanted real help to assist me in my spiritual journey. Or, maybe it wasn't that I wanted help, but I knew in my core that as hard as I had tried, I had been unable to transform myself. I still believed in a much bigger human potential than I was experiencing, but I was clueless how to experience it for myself.

Even though I knew I was not getting anywhere on my own and that I needed some real help, I still was also full of doubt and only half believed that someone who could give me that kind of help really existed. Many of those who were supposed to be something special, I could not recognize or relate to, or if they did seem to have an inner quality, they still did not have any impact on my life. So, why bother?

How does the line in that song go? "What if God was one of us?" Well, what if? I had come to the point where I had decided that even if I met Christ or Buddha, I would probably either fail to recognize the realization in them or would dismiss the realization and assume it was incapable of reaching me. At this point, I had one question, really. How could an enlightened being said to have access to other dimensions help me to become self-realized?

Several months went by, and I gave little thought to Sadhguru, although I do remember having the passing notion that if he really was a guru that had anything to do with me and my life, he would find me.

Perhaps he did. At any rate, a few months later when I was online buying tickets to a Deva Premal concert at the local Unity church in Atlanta, much to my surprise, Sadhguru's picture popped up on their website. He was going to be giving a talk at that Unity church, fifteen minutes from my home, the following week. My natural curiosity was piqued, and I decided to go and check him out.

When I arrived at the church, I chose to sit toward the front of the room, but off to the side so I could get a close look and still be more of an observer than an engaged participant. As fate would have it, after I took my seat, some volunteers went up on the stage and rearranged the setup, positioning Sadhguru's chair directly in front of me. So much for my plans. This was going to be a much closer look than I had intended.

I went to this talk fully guarded, expecting Sadhguru to have plenty of charm, but also believing that he would have no effect on me. I had lived long enough to insulate myself from being unduly influenced by a person's magnetism, be it personal or professional. However, when he walked into the room that night, he was immediately and anciently familiar to me. He had an essence that I knew and have always known. I felt I had known him forever. In addition to my shock at recognizing him, something inside me was completely rattled.

He looked like the original guru, ancient, timeless, serious, and also, how can I put this, twinkly. On top of that, he was strikingly beautiful, turban and all. He wore a long, off-white, raw silk tunic; a beautiful silk, tapestry-type shawl; a saffron-colored turban; and stylish brown trekking sandals. All that was eye-catching, but his was not just a physical beauty. There was a spiritual radiance that permeated his being and filled the room. He had an inner strength that seemed to blend subtlety with tenderness, and it ameliorated the brutal directness of his talk. I had come looking for a mystic, and I wasn't disappointed.

Somehow I knew immediately, even before he spoke, that here was the "something more" I had been looking for. I sensed that he knew what I wanted to know and that he was what I wanted to be. I intuitively felt that he could lead me to "it." There are people you meet who are larger than life. Sadhguru made them seem small.

In speaking, he was articulate, fun, funny, and flawlessly logical. The answers to life's questions poured out of him. He talked about many things, from the mundane and practical aspects of life all the way to the deeper dimensions of existence. He explained how the yoga program he designed, called Isha Yoga, derived from many centuries of yogic wisdom, could be used by anyone to attain wholeness, vitality, personal growth, and self-realization.

He spoke about freedom and how many or most of us have become hostage to external situations. He said, "The one and only reason that you are unhappy is that life is not happening the way you think it should it happen. There are two aspects to this. One is you can go about fixing your life to concur with your thoughts, or you can instantly have the ability to consciously create the kind of thought that you need. If your happiness and your well-being are not subject to anybody or anything, only then you are free. Otherwise, whether you are in prison or walking on the street, you are still a prisoner within yourself."

He also spoke about stress. He said that many people have accepted stress as a way of life and that some people refuse to believe that they do not have to have it. He said, "One is not stressful because of what he is doing; one is stressful because he is a bad manager of himself. He doesn't know how to manage his own systems. That is why he is stressful.

"Everybody believes their job is stressful. You ask the president if his job is stressful, you ask the top executive, and he is also stressful. You ask the office boy, and his job is also stressful! I beg to differ. No job is stressful. Only if you have no control over your own systems are you

stressed. Your body, mind, chemistry, or your life energies are not happening the way you want them to. None
of them are taking instructions from you. If only your
physical, mental, chemical, and energy systems took
instructions from you, would you ever cause any kind of
unpleasantness within yourself? You would be blissful
every moment of your life. Your life would not be at all
enslaved to the external conditions that are subject to a
million different forces. At the same time some are
stressed, others are doing the same jobs joyfully. So, the
question is not at all about the work. If we were good
managers of ourselves, we would become happier as we
grow older; instead, the opposite is true. Children are
bursting forth with happiness," he said, "but most adults
become less and less happy."

That night, Sadhguru spoke plainly about many
things that seemed apparent but that I had not looked at
in that particular way. Just sitting in front of him, there
was a pull that made my spine sit up straighter. His words
cut through layers of old, worn-out thinking that had
been part of my mental state for years. With each new
insight, my desire for more increased. His logic was flaw-
less to the point that it changed my thinking on the spot.
But, it was more than logic. I still don't know why I
immediately trusted Sadhguru, but after he walked into
the room, my suspicions left me and I felt completely at
home and grateful to be there. At the same time, after he

had been speaking only a few minutes, it was as if my mind stopped and I distinctly remember thinking a loud, resounding "Uh-oh." This was what I had been looking for. I had been whining for years about wanting to be free, and now I hoped I meant it. I knew in that moment that all my self-imposed limitations and comforts were suddenly in danger. I had come into the presence of someone who could show me what real freedom is—not the kind of freedom that flaunts authority or hitchhikes or takes drugs for kicks—but a real freedom that liberates from the inside out. I also knew that unless I was serious about wanting to be free, I should not be here. He was not someone who would just look the other way while I remained a prisoner to my habits, thoughts, and misunderstandings—or whatever it was that was holding me back.

In his palpable presence, let alone the words he spoke, I found Sadhguru to be sweet and threatening at the same time. Ever since I was old enough to realize that my seeking and restlessness had an inner, spiritual dimension, I have exposed myself to the words of countless different teachers and traditions. Almost always it seemed that jewels of insights, although inspiring, never seemed to have much lasting effect on me. Coming face to face with Sadhguru was a stark contrast to everyone and everything else. Not everything he said were things you might want to hear, but his words resonated with truth and cut like a scalpel.

The connection I felt was on a different level altogether, and it showed me the limitations of the prior searching I had been doing. As much as I hated to admit it, I had been searching for a live, enlightened being, and here was that and more. What I had found was intensely alive!

Things he said that night haunted me later when I had time to think about them. One comment in particular that stayed with me was, "Every opinion you have about anything can be a limiting identity." Here I was searching for self-realization down every avenue I could find when all along I was limiting myself by attaching to my own opinions.

After the public talk, I learned that there was going to be a more intimate meeting at someone's home with Sadhguru the following evening. Once I confirmed that I was invited, there was no question about whether I would be there. I was excited about getting to see him again so soon. I found myself wondering just what the excitement I was feeling was all about.

Then I realized that perhaps for the very first time I could actually see the possibility of becoming free, free from longing, free from wanting to be something more, free from all compulsiveness, free from the very process of life and death. It now looked like it was a real possibility and not just something I had cooked up or imagined. The veil I had worn all my life as a result of this vague search lifted from my heart. I had pretty much given up hope after all my unsuccessful years of searching; now I was enormously relieved that this possibility of self-realization did indeed exist. The possibility was right in front of me.

Before I went to the meeting the following night, I thought I should take advantage of the time I would have with him there by asking him a specific question that had been disturbing me for many years. After all, how often do you get a private audience with one of India's most renowned mystics?

As the meeting unfolded, however, I completely forgot about my question. I've since been told by other people that this is a common occurrence. Once you're around Sadhguru, his peace is so contagious and his presence so full that questions and problems often disappear.

As I had suspected earlier, however, this guru was not going to allow anyone around him to remain captive to wrong perceptions or conclusions. Over the years, I've learned how to keep others from reading me. This has been a useful skill in the business world, but this skill got me nowhere with Sadhguru. At one point he stopped what he was doing and pointed directly at me. He told me I had a question. He didn't ask me. He told me.

Surprised, I countered, "No, I don't."

As if reading my mind, he said, "Yes, you have a question."

I insisted again, a little more forcefully this time, "No!"

"Just ask your question!" he replied, just as forcefully.

Well, up to that point people had been asking a variety of questions, polite but rather vague queries on a mixture of pseudo-spiritual or mundane stuff. What they needed to do to fix their lives or to amass wealth, regain health, or whatever. I had no interest in furthering the conversation along those lines. Since Sadhguru insisted, I asked the question that had been festering inside me.

"If my mind can produce a beautiful life for me and get me whatever I have wanted," I said, "why am I not able to produce, or find, self-realization by using my mind?" After all the searching I'd done in my life, I honestly thought I would have been enlightened by now. Instead, after all these years, regrettably, not much had happened within me.

He barely even paused before he said, "You can use your mind, but to be effective, your mind must be uncluttered. The mind must be razor sharp. Only if the mind is razor sharp is it useful as tool for your transformation. There is a form of yoga called Jnana Yoga that leads to union through intelligence. It is a difficult path for most people. Very few people have the caliber of intellect that is needed."

To emphasize his point, he picked up a knife that was inserted in a cake someone had brought to the meeting and said, "Think of it this way. Your mind is like a knife that has cut into a cake. When you pull the knife out, it still has cake on it. Similarly, your mind retains the residue of many different past impressions and experiences. All these past impressions are stuck to your mind like cake sticks to a knife."

This made perfect sense even though I now found myself thinking that he was telling me my mind did not work as a tool because it was too dull. What happened? I was always told how smart I was—and I was happy to believe it.

Sadhguru continued, "Right now, you are not able to use your mind to take you to freedom because your mind is cluttered. You have to keep your mind razor sharp and uncluttered. Then you can slice through to freedom using the mind. Then, whatever your mind may enter into, none of it should stick. Only then can the mind be used as a complete tool.

"Doing yoga will remove the cake from the knife, but it is better to use more than just your mind as a tool. You are not just the mind. There are other aspects of you. You also have a body, you have emotions, and you have energy. Using just one of these aspects, like the mind alone, is like traveling somewhere with just one wheel of the car. All four wheels of the car are needed to go there.

Only with all four wheels can you get there. If you use only one aspect as your path, you can still get there but you may become socially incompetent. Being an effective person in the world will probably not be possible if you are driving your car with just one wheel. It will invariably lead to withdrawal and isolation. It is still worth it, but how many would be ready for that kind of life? It is best to use all four aspects. The yoga we are teaching is a combination of all these four things: mind, body, emotions, and energies. Isha Yoga sets all these forces in one direction.

"Our life energies are the most basic and the most powerful aspect of human beings. Though most people are unaware of it, whichever way our energies play, that's the way our bodies and our minds and our emotions play. So, once we get the energies—the fundamentals—moving in one direction, we can make sure that our bodies, emotions, and minds are also moving in that direction.

"Different people's energies, minds, emotions, and bodies function in different ways. A guru is one who knows what is needed for each individual. There has been so much emphasis on live gurus because they can mix the right combination for each person. The reason Isha Yoga works so effectively for everyone is that it uses every aspect of you to help you grow, not just your mind."

After the meeting, I approached the guru as he was walking out of the room. "Sadhguru, how did you know I had a question?" I asked.

"It was written all over you," he said. So much for my poker face!

While I was trying to figure out in what way my question could have been so obvious, he patiently explained, "Such questions are powerful. An unanswered question can kill people. In this world, most people do not have genuine questions. Their questions usually are only of entertainment value. They ask questions to amuse themselves or to settle their curiosity. It makes them feel intellectual, which is what they aspire to.

"If you have a genuine question, however, you cannot rest until it is answered or resolved. You cannot forget it. Even if you bury it deep, it will bring restlessness and even disease. If you bury it too deep, then you will see that every cell in your body will scream that question.

"Questions of this kind are my business, you know," he added and smiled.

As we talked further, he made a few comments that revealed a surprising understanding of my nature— surprising given that I had seen him for the first time just the night before. As much as I hated to admit it, I felt a bit unnerved at how perceptive and accurate his comments about me were. Among other things, he told me I was in danger of wasting my life to "laziness and complacency."

I knew this was true. I only did what came easy to me, never challenging myself. I was the one looking for effortless bliss, and I enjoyed my comfortable lifestyle.

He then told me to come to India in August, the following month, for a program he would be giving. Immediately I balked; there was no way. I could almost feel myself physically backing up. As much as I wanted to take a class with him as soon as possible, I could not wrap my mind around going to India. I was simply not ready for a trip of this magnitude. I had major health concerns. I could pull it together for three or four hours a day to show up for work, but beyond that, I couldn't even walk across the room without feeling like I was going to pass out, like I was dragging a bag of bricks behind me. Among other things, I had hyperthyroidism and low blood pressure of 75/35. Just walking across the room made me feel dizzy and faint, and I was told I was at high risk for a heart attack. I did not talk about it much, but it was pretty bad. I had been to India ten years before when I was in perfect health and had still gotten violently ill. I seemed to have been a magnet for every germ that was out there. Consequently, I decided I was never going to go back to India even though I had for years fantasized some sort of a distant connection to the land of yogis.

Besides, I suspected that India would be oppressively hot in August.

I told him about my previous experience and how precarious my health was. He was quiet for a minute then said it would be okay for me to come and that I would not be sick while I was there.

Still I resisted. Even though I wanted to go, I had too many doubts and fears about being able to handle such a trip. I decided to wait and take his class the next time he came to the United States. This decision, however, did little to calm a new sense of unease I was feeling.

Here's the thing. I'd sincerely asked for some help. Help showed up and the first thing I did was say no. I felt like I was flunking out even before I've gotten through the door. I couldn't even do the first thing. What would happen with the second thing? Would I even get a second chance? I normally really involve myself in a big way if I am interested in something, yet here was something I really wanted and I was backing away. I was very concerned that even if I had found the guidance I was looking for, I had found it much too late. Perhaps, given my age and health limitations, I might not be able to do whatever it was that was necessary for me to attend his classes, let alone transform.

At that time, I had no way of knowing how trustworthy Sadhguru's words were. He looked like someone who was bothered by nothing, particularly heat or travel, so I figured he could not appreciate how difficult a summer trip to India would be for me.

Although I declined his initial invitation to go to India, I quickly became very focused on learning whatever I could from Sadhguru as soon as possible. In Isha Yoga, the system developed by Sadhguru, the basic program is known as Inner Engineering, a technology that offers a scientifically structured program to help individuals establish optimal physical, mental, and emotional health and vitality, and to prepare the practitioners for deeper levels of spiritual awareness. In the West, many of us have been exposed to various types of yoga exercise, such as Hatha Yoga. In Isha Yoga, the physical postures are taught in order for you to be able to access the higher dimensions. The postures are designed to get you comfortable in your body for sitting and to purify your body and make it more subtle so that these other dimensions become available to you. Although Sadhguru's foundation is based in India, he offers programs around the world. In Isha Yoga there are highly trained instructors who have undergone a very rigorous training for many years under Sadhguru's supervision. Somehow this training allows them to learn how to keep themselves aside and function as conduits to deliver Sadhguru's presence and energy. I have heard any number of people vouch that the teachers' programs are just as good as Sadhguru's and that the participants feel his presence even though he is not physically there.

I planned to take the next program he gave in the U.S. in whatever city it was given, but I did not have to travel because six months later he had a program very close to where I lived in Atlanta. I took two of his classes here in America, and he continued to impress me with the depth of his insight and his ability to open up possibilities within me. In fact, the following February I did go all the way to India for the advanced program that was only offered there. As Sadhguru promised, my health was fine. I spent nine weeks in India that next year and was even able to do a Himalayan trek (which would have been physically impossible for me a year earlier) with him and a group of meditators. I spent two months in India the following year, and I have been going to India at least once a year ever since.

When I began Isha Yoga, I was taking four prescription medications daily. It sounds like a lot, but I was surprised it wasn't more! I had a variety of things wrong with my health. The hyperthyroidism I had was the incurable Graves' disease. I had a multitude of other things that were off with my system. I had chronic fatigue, allergies, a constantly queasy stomach, deep physical body pain, and chronic insomnia. My health had gotten so bad that it was embarrassing to me. It had been getting progressively out of whack for several years. Frankly, I was feeling 60 percent dead. It was taking enormous effort to keep functioning.

When I did take Sadhguru's program, even though most everyone found it blissful, I had so much physical pain that just sitting still was very difficult for me. Because of this, there was no opportunity whatsoever at first for me to benefit from the more spiritual aspects of the practices. I was concerned that I might be the one person this process would not work for.

The peak experiences happening to other people did not happen to me, and even though I felt extremely disappointed, somehow I stuck with the practices. As I said, I am often undisciplined and lazy, and I had to ignore my own whining. I knew that if anything was going to transform me, this was it. Something had very obviously worked for Sadhguru, and I knew he would not waste his time with these programs if they did not work. The practices are a unique system of bringing balance and intensity to one's body, mind, emotion, and energy; they consist of powerful breathing techniques and meditation among other things. Even in the state of health I was in, the practices were doable. I have to admit that my morning practice leaves me with such a certain kind of serenity and blissfulness that lasts throughout the day that I do not want to miss it for anything. I kept at them day after day, and as a result, many things changed—and they actually changed really fast.

I was off most of the prescription medication in three months. When my doctor read my blood work, he said, quite uncharacteristically for a man of few words, "This is astonishing! This is astonishing! This is astonishing!"

That is no exaggeration. He said it three times, just like that, and he added that he had never seen anyone as hyperthyroid as I, for as long as I had been, get this well this quickly. He is not some crystal-wearing, New-Age doctor, either, but a well-respected endocrinologist with a wall full of degrees and awards from the halls of traditional academia. I had also suffered with allergies and other symptoms for several years. Now they, too, were gone.

In addition to becoming healthy, I have experienced for myself many of the things Sadhguru promised in the first class. I used to be a big worrier. Now it is such a relief not to be in a constant state of concern about the worst thing I could imagine happening. I was having a conversation recently with my father about some of his concerns for himself, me, and the world and he said, "Nothing really bothers you, does it?"

"No, nothing really does, at least not the way it did before," I answered.

"I wish I could be like that," he said.

Over the years I had acquired the same kind of worried mind my father had. It would go on a seek-and-destroy mission, looking for the next thing to worry about. Now most of the time, I have a deep, consistent sense of joy, although my mind is still more active than I want it to be. I don't dwell on difficult things so much and tend to do what I can to make changes without adding any personal drama. If there's a problem, I just try to figure out what to do about it. I don't want to waste this moment. Challenging situations still happen, but I do not lose sleep over them. Sadhguru has said that peace of mind is only the beginning, not the goal. That was exciting to me because even though my health was much better and my mind had settled down, I came for something else.

CHAPTER THREE
Our Week Begins: Sadhguru Arrives

"I want you to know the power, the liberation of another kind of science—the inner science—through which you can become the master of your own destiny."
—Sadhguru

On a sunny August afternoon, I drove to the Atlanta airport to wait for Sadhguru's arrival. I was to be his host at my lake house in the mountains of North Carolina, and this would be the first time I would have unlimited access to the guru whose teachings I had been getting to know. I felt unbelievably excited, but the prospect was also daunting. Things with him are often totally unpredictable, no matter how much you try to prepare for every eventuality.

It had been three years since I'd met Sadhguru in Atlanta. Even though I had enjoyed quite a bit of time spent with him over the past few years, I still found myself with a variety of emotions every time I went to see him: big enthusiasm combined with a bit of edgy anticipation. But it's a transitory problem, for as soon as I am with him, I'm completely absorbed in the situation. Many times I find myself sinking deeper and deeper into the stillness of his presence, but at other times my curious mind doesn't want to miss an opportunity to get my endless questions answered.

Sadhguru and his assistant Leela were coming to be my guests at my lake house for an entire week. Sadhguru had first become acquainted with the lake the previous year, when he stayed at my place for one night. I could tell he really liked it. Since that time, I had been bugging him to come back. As it turned out, he periodically withdraws into seclusion to attend to some type of inner work. Since the lake house is nothing if not secluded, it was the perfect setting.

Leela had been with Sadhguru for almost fifteen years. Trained as an engineer, she has practically unlimited options for her life, yet she has chosen to serve as a fulltime volunteer for Isha Yoga. She assists Sadhguru in much of his day-to-day work in the United States. Despite her many responsibilities, she is easily one of the most unruffled people I have ever met. With a keen mind and a dry sense of humor, she often makes her point in a most penetrating and unexpected way.

As much as I love to share the lake house, I had no doubt that extending my hospitality to Sadhguru would be a unique experience. Although the serene confidence that characterizes photographs of him might give the impression that Sadhguru is an entirely gentle, other-worldly figure, in person he would be better described as an active volcano: dynamic, forceful, unpredictable, and with an explosive sense of energy. When I'm with him, I never know what is going to happen next. I felt entirely clueless about how to make this the ideal week because he had not been particularly forthcoming about his plans. I only knew that he wanted to spend most of the time in silence.

I hoped I would be able to do the right thing, whatever that was. Always the perfectionist, I not only asked Leela for advice beforehand, I also e-mailed Sadhguru's *ashram* in India for suggestions. Both requests were met with the same disarmingly uninformative advice: something simple and comfortable would be just fine. I was looking for details and trying to be prepared for anything (grocery lists, etc.), but got nowhere. It seems to be always this way with him. You can never be completely prepared no matter how hard you try because things are constantly changing.

When I arrived at the designated waiting area in the airport that afternoon, I found a large and glowingly enthusiastic group of people representing all ages and cultures waiting to see Sadhguru, even though his travel plans had not been formally announced. There was a buzz of excitement in the air that caught the attention of everyone, even the normally unflappable security guards. The enthusiasm and shining eyes of so many people, young and old, seemed to create a living sense of anticipation, a sizzle and crackle of energy as if we were all conductors along a vast power line. At the heart of the excitement, it seemed to me, was the unspoken but potent knowledge that in his presence a possibility beyond all that we knew was alive and available.

Standing there, I remembered that before I met and got to know Sadhguru, this scene at the airport would have made me uneasy and would have raised multiple red flags. I would have found many of the people too reverential, their admiration too uncomfortable. My quick-to-disbelieve radar would have popped up and registered concern, yet here I was, happy and enjoying the excitement around me. It was evidence of how far I had come, how much I had come to believe that this guru was the real thing, and how much I valued knowing Sadhguru and having him in my life.

I lingered on the fringe of the crowd, simply soaking in the scene. I saw that many people brought gifts for the guru. Several held bouquets of flowers to offer him, and one man held a picture he had painted. Others held specific things Sadhguru was known to like. There was a jar of spicy hot pickles, a big bag of special handmade soap, and even a Frisbee, which this athletic guru likes to throw when he has a free minute.

As the time for Sadhguru's 4:30 p.m. arrival approached, people were finding the right spots to get their first glimpses of him. At precisely the appointed time, the plane touched down, and soon disembarking passengers began to stream past us. And then we caught sight of him walking calmly, his serene, glowing, caramel-skinned face in sharp contrast to the harried expressions of those surrounding him. As often happens, I felt a brief shock. His appearance is extraordinary. He is both old and young. He had a gray/white beard that reached to the middle of his chest, yet he wore classic aviator style sunglasses and tan jeans. We were from the same generation. He was, in fact, my contemporary. Both of us had grown up listening to the Beatles and the Rolling Stones.

As if oblivious to the rushing flow of hurrying travelers around him, Sadhguru moved with a warm smile toward the group that had come to greet him. He acknowledged each person, some with a smile, and others with a nod, some with a hug, and others with a piercing comment that cut to the quick.

The long flight had not numbed his whimsical sense of humor. Someone asked, "How was your flight, Sadhguru?" He replied quickly, "Oh, they didn't let me fly! I was just sitting around." Then he threw back his head and gave his usual hearty, deep laugh.

Even though he had been traveling for the past thirty-six hours and still had many miles more to go before he could rest, he appeared unhurried and truly present as he interacted with those who had come out to see him, answering their questions with his full attention and briefly talking with volunteers about the details of his agenda.

This was not the first time I had seen Sadhguru interact with people in a public setting, and I've never seen him pull back from others to attend to any of his own needs. It's as if when surrounded by those who come to him for guidance and instruction, he has no personal concerns. I've seen him patiently tend to each person waiting in long lines to speak with him even though he has not eaten or slept; even though he must work for hours when he is finished. Every question, even those that are trivial, is answered with words that reveal a genuine depth and profundity. More than one person has told me they would ask him a seemingly ordinary question only to have his response touch their real question, often deeply held and unspoken. One time I mentioned this to him, and he replied, "I always answer the person, not the question."

For almost an hour, Sadhguru continued to speak with person after person, exchanging greetings, joking amicably, listening intently. Finally, from the soap lady to the Frisbee guy, everyone seemed happy at this opportunity to see him again. The energy radiating sun-like from him left a glow on every face. After the last goodbye, Sadhguru and I walked leisurely to the baggage claim. As we waited for his bags, I took a look at one of the gifts he had been given, a book about the mystic Sufi poet, Rumi. I knew enough about Rumi to know that his poetry celebrates a love affair with the divine, so I asked Sadhguru, "Is love the ultimate possibility that one can seek?"

Just then his bag appeared on the carousel, and as he reached for it, I assumed he missed my question. With his bag safely in hand, we headed for my car. The wheels of his suitcase creaked and groaned on the pavement, their noise echoing off the cinderblock walls of the brightly lit parking deck as we walked to the car.

Knowing Sadhguru is as much a man of motion as he is of stillness, I asked him if he wanted to drive. It is a well-known fact that he loves to drive—and fast—but after such a long trip, I thought he might want to rest. Not a chance. Laughing, I rolled my eyes as I handed over the keys. I should have known he wouldn't let the opportunity pass. I took the passenger seat and strapped the seatbelt on securely, reflecting one more time on the guru's reputation as a driver of vehicles (and of people).

In India, where speed limits seem nonexistent, he is known for pushing his car—not to mention his students—to the limit.

He inserted the key into the ignition and then looked intently at me and asked, "How fast can I go?"

I don't know why he bothered to ask; it was really never up to me. Squealing out of the parking garage, he probably couldn't have heard me even if I had answered him.

The trip from Atlanta to the mountains normally takes close to three hours. But after only a few gear-stripping minutes, we were out of the city and well on our way to setting a new trip record. I reflected on how absurd the notion of an Indian yoga master speeding down Interstate 85 in a BMW convertible might be to most people (including most state troopers), but then I just smiled and relaxed. I knew that I was riding shotgun on what would be an incredible journey—and not just while we were in the car.

I'd had plenty of experience with Sadhguru's hell-for-leather driving style in India, so it seemed like a fair question to ask him, "Sadhguru, why this passion with engines and speed?"

"Oh," he responded, smiling, "I am passionate about every thing in life; driving is one of the few things that are left now due to the demands of time because of the work I have taken up."

He changed lanes with dexterous care before adding, "I have always liked vehicles of all kinds, starting when I was a child. At one point, my biggest dream was to have a bicycle. When I finally got it, I spent a lot of time on it. I would always have new tires on my bike. When they were a little worn out, I gave them away. It was not flamboyance, you know. I did not care what the bike looked like. The ride had a different feeling when it had new tires on it, and that's the kind of stuff I cared for."

"I know how you drive," I said, "so I can only imagine that you wore through lots of tires for your bike. Where did you get the money to keep buying new tires?"

Sadhguru laughed and said, "I made sure I had enough odd jobs and enterprises to make money when I was a kid."

"Like what?" I asked. I was trying to get a feel for what a kid raised in India might do to get money.

"There was a research campus that paid big money to have the poisonous snakes removed from their grounds. They paid different prices for removal of the different sized cobras and vipers. I would also catch parrots. I wanted to be able to keep my bike up and fund my cycling expeditions, so I was delighted to have found that job. Besides, no one else would or could to do it. I would perform actions that were considered risky and take any challenge I could find for excitement or money."

I was glad that Sadhguru's reminiscing had expanded beyond his love for speed into a rare glimpse into his childhood—but catching poisonous snakes?

He continued in that vein, "The other kids were often daring me to climb things," he said. "I could climb anything. With the money I made, I was able to fund bicycle trips for ten to fifteen boys for four to five days at a time. That's big funding for a ten-year-old. That's how I spent my money. I never went to restaurants or cared about new clothes. I had too many outdoor interests."

Another way that Sadhguru expressed his love for cars was through his attentive knowledge of the various cars we passed on the interstate. As he drove along, he noticed and commented on such details as the model numbers, engine specifications, gear ratios, and transmission capabilities down to minute performance details of cars we passed. He'd point out the year in which this or that automobile was made and when design changes were implemented. It seemed to me that nothing escaped his notice.

"You certainly seem to have an encyclopedic knowledge of cars," I said as we sped along. He didn't acknowledge the comment, but instead changed the subject. "I also loved airplanes," he said. "I was desperate to fly. I almost joined the Indian Air Force because that would get me to fly. A few of us built a hang glider. I took the maiden flight and jumped off a nearby hill in the rickety contraption. Instead of soaring in the sky, I quickly crashed into a ravine below. Not only was the hang glider broken, but it broke both my ankles, too," he said and laughed uproariously with his contagious, bellowing laugh.

"Wow, I bet your parents loved that one," I said wryly.

"Yes, my father was always concerned that I never had any fear about anything."

I smiled and shook my head. Fast cars, fast planes, poisonous snakes, and who knows what else. Fearlessness and a love for engineering seemed to coalesce in him. I thought about how his love for the gas pedal echoes a similar love he has for accelerating the spiritual evolution of those who study with him. Of course, it made perfect sense that the yoga he teaches is a kind of engineering: spiritual engineering.

Sadhguru's life seems to have a more clear purpose than anyone else's I have known, yet his youth had its own share of wildness and meandering. I wondered just how much more control he exercised over his life than the average person. What drove this fast-driving mystic? Did destiny have anything to do with it? For that matter, does destiny drive anyone?

"Sadhguru," I asked as the speeding white lines of the highway lulled me into a hypnotic, receptive state, "is there such a thing as destiny? Just how much control do we actually have over our lives?"

I take pride in being a focused and goal-oriented person, and I know that this trait has been a great help in my life (particularly in terms of my career), but despite my focus, I also knew how much in my life eluded my control. I wanted to know just how far I could push myself in terms of managing every corner of my experience. And since I approached life from a spiritual perspective, I also wanted to know what kind of unseen forces such as karma, the energies of cause and effect that pulse through our lives, play a role in determining what specific events are destined to happen (or not happen). Are we at the mercy of our destiny, or can even that be changed?

He paused before answering. "Now what you are really asking is if life is already pre-fixed. That's the question. This question comes up because certain things are happening in your life, and even though you are trying to push it one way, it is often going another way. That is the reason for the question.

"So, is this destiny? As you know, external situations are controlled by many, many forces. Right now, we are driving in this car, and this situation is controlled by gravity, the movement of the planet—its rotation and revolution—and atomic forces, and any number of things. There are also forces at work well beyond present levels of perception and understanding. We only understand them to some extent, and to that extent we can control them.

"For example, one can steer a car, make sure there is enough gas, and obey the rules of the road. Those things are under one's control, but gravity is not under our control. But our understanding of situations has hugely improved in the last fifty years. We now think less about destiny and more about things happening by intent. Do you see this?"

He paused expectantly. Clearly, he was not asking a rhetorical question.

"Yes," I said. "I definitely don't think along the lines that if it is meant to be it will be, the way my grandmother used to think."

"So," he continued, "in the next one hundred years, if our perception and understanding is greatly enhanced, you will see us less and less at the mercy of destiny. Most situations will be in our hands. It is beginning to happen, slowly, step by step, isn't it? Still, we do not understand all the forces working upon this particular situation right now, so everything we don't understand, we say is God's will. That is a childish explanation for all that you are unable to perceive and understand. It's an easy way of washing it off. We label it this way because we have not understood the realities of life properly.

"Right now, we are doing a major project in the rural areas in South India. You know I have been involved with rural people since I was young, but when I really got there and saw .everything that was happening, I was amazed that in the twenty-first century, when a government medical dispensary is not more than five kilometers away in any village, every year more than seventy thousand children lose their vision simply because of something as treatable as conjunctivitis.

"Conjunctivitis does not take away vision; the children are just scratching out their eyeballs. If they just leave their eyes alone for another four days without medicine, they will be okay, but the children are unable to bear the itch. Just two drops of an antibiotic and their vision need not vanish. Do you think that is destiny or something that we can change?"

"Definitely it's something that can and should be changed," I answered.

"Whatever your destiny is right now," he continued, "it is self-created, but unfortunately, you are creating it unconsciously. It is written by you and nobody else. The creator has given you perfect freedom. He has put his own self into you. Your destiny is written by you. It is only because of feelings of helplessness that people are talking so much about destiny. You can also create your destiny consciously. I want you to know the power, the liberation, of another kind of science—the inner science—the yogic science through which you can become the master of your own destiny.

"You have not yet understood the enormity of being human. If you take a human being to his full height, the divine will be a part of his life. If you have mastery over your physical body, 10 to 15 percent of your life and destiny is under your control. If you have sufficient mastery over your mind, 40 to 60 percent of your life and destiny will be under your control. If you have complete mastery over your life energies, 100 percent of your life and destiny will be under your control.

"The whole science of yoga is just to work on these three levels: body, mind, and energy. Any human being can explore his capabilities to the fullest only when he exists in a state where there are no issues of his own. There are no internal issues, either of body, thought, or emotion. It is only in this state that he can find expression to all that he is. All that we are doing in the form of spiritual process is just that. You decide where you want to go, the next course and destination. It is in your hands. As there is a physical science for external well-being, there is an inner science, a yogic science. With this, you can take your destiny 100 percent into your own hands. You can take 100 percent of the very process of life into your hands. The very way that you are born you can decide. The very womb that you are born in can be chosen by you consciously. That is the extent to which you can have mastery over your own life.

"Your birth, the very process of life and your death, can be your choice. You can create your life the way you want it. Even now it is your choice, but you are choosing it unconsciously. One can choose consciously, also. If you do not take your destiny into your hands, you live accidentally. When you live accidentally, anxiety is very natural. Almost 90 percent of the world is anxious all the time. This is simply because people make no effort to take their lives into their own hands; the way it happens, it happens."

"If we are unconsciously creating our destiny right now, how is it happening? Is it our thoughts, or our actions, or our past actions?" I asked.

"Who you are right now," he replied, "your whole personality, everything that you are, is a complex accumulation of your impressions of life itself. This is like your software. This is what is referred to as karma. It is the volume of your impressions. Everything you have perceived has imprinted itself on your mind and even on your energy. The very way your body behaves, the very way your energies behave, is a result of the past impressions of your karma. The very way you move your body is programmed. So what you call karma is the sum of the vast store of impressions you have taken as your software. Because of these impressions, you develop certain tendencies. These are unconscious tendencies.

"Your body, your mind, your emotions, your energies, everything works according to these tendencies that
evolve because of the vast store of impressions. This is
the influence of karma on your life. Unless one rises to a
certain pitch of awareness and has a certain mastery over
oneself, one is always being pushed and pulled by these
tendencies that have been created unconsciously. Even
though you are being pushed in a certain direction, all
this was created by you, no one else but you."

"So if we created it, can we undo—or avoid—that
which we created?" I asked excited at the prospect. "Or,
can we change it with awareness? Or, are there some
experiences that are definitely destined to happen?"

Sadhguru answered, "Right now, yes. There are many
things that are bound to happen because these tendencies
are far deeper than your mental determination. If you
determine to go in a certain way, there are many things
you can change. Certain fundamental things will find
their own way. However, once a person has a certain mastery over his life energies, he can completely change the
course of his life.

"Now we are talking about creating the same thing
consciously. The very fact that a person turns spiritual
when he says, 'I am seeking liberation' means he wants to
take the course of his life into his hands. You want to take
your destiny into your hands. With the very first step of
yoga you are trying to take charge of some part of you,

starting with the body, the breath, and then the mind and the energy. You are going step by step. It is more than just about being free from suffering. You can definitely change the course of your destiny."

"Sadhguru," I said, "all those things you said in the program that would happen if I stuck to these practices have happened to me. Life now has a certain sense of ease to it. I actually like the practices. Also, so many little and also not so little things are completely gone now. The constant state of anxiety I was in is now gone. Still, I do not necessarily feel that I am closer to taking more of my life into my hands."

"Cheryl, definitely you are taking it into your own hands. You were in a bad state of health when I met you. Even your eyes were sunk. If you had not stuck to your practices, you were on the road to a major disaster. If you had not stuck to your yoga, by now you would be much worse. Ask your doctor where you were heading. Now all that has changed. So, did you take life into your hands? You are on your feet, able to do everything far better than before. Definitely that part of your life has been taken into your hands. Ask your doctor. He will confirm what I am saying. Once you are physically unhealthy to that point, everything crashes. Now all that is fixed, your energy is up. Just look at how your health has improved. So, all those things you unknowingly took into your hands the minute you took your physical health into your hands."

Looking young and exuberant with his hair tied back in a ponytail, Sadhguru lowered his sunglasses and looked at me with those ancient, all-knowing eyes. I knew he did not want me to miss this point that what has happened to me did not happen by accident. Beyond all predictions by medical experts, what he said was true. Before I began to practice Isha Yoga, my health was in bad shape. It took enormous effort just to keep functioning at work. It was all I could do to get through each day, pretending that nothing was wrong. By the time I got home in the evening, I was not able to do much of anything. I felt completely zapped, without one drop of energy left. Now, by comparison, I feel wonderful and light.

"So, what do we have to do to fully take our destiny into our own hands?" I asked. "I heard someone ask you about how to control her thoughts, and she talked about how her thoughts ran on endlessly, out of her control, in many different directions without any apparent reason. That seems to be true for most of us. I heard you say that we cannot control our thoughts when we identify ourselves as so many things: our bodies, our minds, jobs, and families. It sounded like you said that all that has something to do with our controlling our destiny. Can you explain?"

"The moment you are identified with many things that you are not, then you cannot stop the thoughts. Starting with the physical body, which is an accumulation, the mind, the emotions, things, people. You have taken on so many false identifications. They run on endlessly.

"People do not understand the relationship between these false identities and themselves. You may know happiness in this state. You may know some joy because of some external situations, but just being yourself in an absolutely pleasant way is not possible for most people. Happiness in this state is because of something external. It is not the way you are."

"Sadhguru, most everyone I know is mainly looking for a perfect life," I said. "The perfect mate, beautiful scenery, unlimited wealth. I like those things too, but I know we are selling ourselves short. I still feel there is so much more than that."

"Definitely there is more. Once you do the necessary *sadhana* (spiritual work), you have a certain amount of mastery over your body, mind, and energies. If one wants to pursue a spiritual destiny, a lot more control is needed. A lot more mastery is needed. But, if you are only seeking material well-being, just a certain amount of mastery is needed, and very easily you can achieve these things."

"I still feel we are really selling ourselves short by only trying to have a nice life," I said.

"Even with a little mastery over your mind and body, you can easily achieve those things. If you intensify and enhance your life energies beyond a certain pitch that will make your energies more dominant than your mind and your body, then you can effortlessly create what you want. What you want in the physical plane in the world will come and fall at your feet without you investing your life upon them. This should not take much of your time at all. Successful people are those people who have a certain amount of mastery over their minds. They are able to apply themselves in a certain way more than other people. However, it is best if you transcend the compulsive nature of desiring; otherwise, you will throw this planet off balance by creating too many unnecessary things," Sadhguru said.

"I am frustrated," I said, "because once I became focused in my life, I was able to make a lot of what I wanted to happen externally happen, yet I have not had any luck making anything spiritual happen."

"You have only been able to make small things happen. You have not yet been able to make big things happen. You need to be able to make big, big things happen. If you can for one moment experience that the source of creation is within you and shift your whole focus to yourself," he said, "you can rewrite your own destiny."

Certainly, I had not been able to make big, big things happen. Sadhguru was reminding me how important it is that my health has improved so much. I did not mean to undervalue that. If you don't have your health, it takes a front seat to everything. Because I lacked stamina and had so much pain, the Isha programs at first had been very difficult for me. Because that is gone, I am now able to experience more of the subtle aspects of the yoga, but this has just added to the intensity of wanting to become all that is possible.

I had barely noticed the scenery blurring by when we were on the interstate, but now we were on a two-lane highway and approaching the North Georgia Mountains. Lush green fields, which were dotted with neatly rolled, harvested, golden hay, and we were surrounded by a hazy mountain backdrop. At one point, we pulled over to drop the convertible top. It was ninety-five degrees and the sky was white when we left Atlanta, but here it was at least ten degrees cooler and without the humidity. The sky was a beautiful, brilliant blue.

As we drove on, he continued to address my concerns.

"First, who you are should be established," he said. "Your focus is scattered because what you call 'myself' is what you are identified with: your body, your mind, your house, your car, your husband, your child, your pet, your education, your business, your power, and all your other accumulations. If I stripped you of all these identities, you would feel like a nobody. So, what you refer to as 'myself' is spread around you right now. When I say 'you,' I mean just you. Not this car, not this trip, not this week, not your child, not something else—just you. If this 'you' remains unidentified with anything other than what it really is, you can rewrite your destiny whichever way you want. Right now, you are a scattered being. There is no you; there is just an accumulated past. You still have to gather up all this mess and put it aside.

"As long as you are identified with all these things you have accumulated, you are a crowd, and the crowd's destiny is always predestined. Once you become an individual, you cannot be divided anymore. Indivisible means infinite. You can make fractions out of everything except the infinite. That which can be fragmented will not know absolute stability. What that means is, you are piecemeal; just holding yourself together is a feat. It is no wonder that people are an anxious mess. Once you become a true individual, not identified with anything, your destiny is yours. I want you to understand this."

I really wanted to understand it, too. Listening to him speak, I wondered how I was scattering my focus without realizing it. I was no longer full of anxiety, but my spiritual destiny still definitely wasn't in my hands. As he says, Sadhguru answers not just the question, but the person. I knew this definitely applied to me and I wondered, Am I still too identified with my body, mind, house, car, husband, child, pet, education, business, power, the list of things he mentioned? How do I stay completely involved in my life without being identified? Some people leave their lives to become yogis. I wanted to become enlightened within the structure I had set up. Was it possible? He says that you can live in the world and be liberated. How? How do you live that experience of being "indivisible"?

Sadhguru continued: "The more you get enslaved by the logical process of the mind, the more and more you aspire to be exclusive. The whole society today is encouraging exclusivity. Exclusiveness means that you are separating yourself from life. You are making a cocoon of your own. The need for exclusiveness has come from a deep sense of insecurity. Exclusiveness and insecurity feed upon each other. This whole phenomenon of exclusiveness and insecurity that is ruling a large part of humanity is purely psychological. It has no existential elements."

I thought about how true that was for our culture here in the United States. We live in our separate worlds, in our exclusive neighborhoods, keeping out anyone we don't like or want. It isn't just the rich who do this. Even in poor neighborhoods, it can be dangerous to be an outsider. We allow a very limited number of people into our circles. Could this self-imposed isolation be keeping us from truly living?

"Your physical body and the life within are effortlessly inclusive. The physical body has been picked up and is on loan from the planet, but you made it into yourself. With every inhalation and exhalation, you are transacting with the whole world. The energy within is always one with everything, so your exclusiveness is purely a mental boundary. In other words, you have a mind that is not in line with all life. When your mind is not in line with the life you are, you have become unwilling for the process of life to happen at its peak. This unwillingness is purely psychological.

"Every cell in you is striving to exist and thrive. When you do not know this, you feel mentally depressed and you may feel like you want to die. Close your mouth and hold your nose and see what happens. You will see that everything in you will make a clear statement that it wants to live. As the life process is a process of inclusion, if you set forth the psychological process of exclusion and create a deep sense of unwillingness toward the life process itself, then mentally you are working against the very life that you are. This is fundamentally the source of all suffering. If you align the mind with the rest of you, then mind can be made absolutely inclusive. With this inclusiveness, you become blissful. With this inclusiveness, your life process becomes willing. Whatever you do willingly is your heaven and whatever you do unwillingly is your hell. When one is all-inclusive, blissfulness is a natural state.

"Yoga means knowing and experiencing everything as a part of yourself. Modern science has proved beyond a doubt that everything is one energy. Religions are screaming that God is everywhere. Whether you say God is everywhere or everything is one energy, you are saying the same thing from two different contexts. A scientist has mathematically deduced this reality. He has not experienced it. His realization is intellectual. It does not transform his life. A religious person just believes it. A yogi is one who is unwilling to settle either for deductions or for belief systems. He wants to experience and know it. In that sense, yoga is a technology of taking a person from his individuality to his universality, to knowing and experiencing existence as himself.

"Patanjali, who is considered to be the father or assimilator of yoga, said this very beautifully. When he began the Yoga Sutras, he said, 'And now, yoga.' What he meant was that now you have tried everything—tasted money, power, wealth, love, pleasure, and you even did the drugs," Sadhguru said and laughed, "and nothing really worked. It was all fine, but it did not bring you any great sense of fulfillment. When you know this, you are ready for yoga."

I thought about all that I had experienced in my life: so many moments of pleasure and fun. I also remembered when I realized my business was going to be a success. After not having any money, finally I was able to buy my own house, go to the restaurants I wanted to go to, travel and do whatever I wanted. I thought I'd finally made it. But, it was never enough. Nothing in my life, no matter how wonderful, ever completely satisfied me.

"For the most part, many people enjoy all those things only because everyone is not able to have them. That is the only reason they are considered special. If everyone in the world was a billionaire, you would no longer care about being a billionaire. You are often only enjoying things because you think they are special or unique. This is not real joy. When you have gotten to the place where you realize that all these things, no matter what they are, do not bring you real joy in an absolute way, then you are ready for yoga. That's why Patanjali starts the yoga sutras with 'And now, yoga.'

"We can walk through life untouched. When we walk, we want to walk on a pleasant street. No problem with that. So, let's walk on a pleasant street, but don't invest yourself in it. If you invest yourself in it, you will become the pavement everyone walks on. So, invest yourself completely within yourself.

"If your destiny is in your own hands, will you choose bondage or freedom? You will choose freedom because the deepest longing of every life is to be free from the very processes we refer to as life and death. So, once your destiny is happening in awareness, the next step will just happen by itself because the life within you has the intelligence to choose freedom, not bondage. Only because your destiny is being created in unawareness do you go about weaving bondages about yourself."

I nodded, silently drifting into my own thoughts. I understood that I had always been identified with my body and mind. Even though most of us believe in something after the death of the body, we all still identify with our bodies. I could understand this, even though my comprehension of it did not seem to change my experience. I even knew that my mind could not be me, since I knew I could not always listen to what it was saying. To also understand that I have added even more false identifications was something I had been unaware of.

Before I knew it, we reached the turn up to the mountains of North Carolina. I still had much I wanted to ask Sadhguru about destiny, but I also wanted to make sure I would be able to be as helpful as possible while he was here. So I asked, "What will you be doing this week? Is there some way I can help?"

"Are you a good cook?" He asked and laughed.

I frowned and admitted, "Not really. I can put a few things together, but I would not call it cooking." I definitely did not want to risk cooking for him, especially since I knew that his assistant, Leela, who was meeting us at my mountain house, could do this much better.

"Then you cannot be of much use to me," he said and laughed again.

"No, really, is there any way I can assist you in your work? Is there anything that you need?" I asked. I wasn't sure what the nature of his work was, and truthfully, I suppose I was fishing for some kind of clue. I had heard a lot about how important the mystical part of his work is and how little he spoke about it.

I did not think he would explain, but after a long pause he said, "Cheryl, you could say I have a very large family. They are spread around the world, and sometimes they need a little tending to. Many of them depend on me for their well-being. There are also other aspects to it that may be too much for your logical mind to digest. You may be surprised to know that I have initiated even more people that I have not met than I have met. Physical distance does not matter here.

"Besides, people not only seek spiritual guidance from me; they are also looking for other kinds of help. There are also many sick people that I need to attend to. Sometimes when it is time, I help people with their transition."

This is definitely over my head, but I wish I could understand everything about him, I thought as Sadhguru fell silent. He seemed not to want to say anymore about it. So, changing the subject, I asked him how Leela got to be lucky enough to be his assistant and, thereby, to spend so much time with him.

"You know, when I travel, I travel with those people who are quiet," he answered. "I do not need anyone's company. I am at my best when I am alone, but my work is a constant and deep involvement with people. Through the day there are many, many people around me, and I do not hesitate for a moment to be deeply involved in their lives, as I have no fear of entanglement. My involvement with people is absolute.

"When I am in private spaces, there are a few people who are allowed to be around me and assist me. I choose those who have imbibed a certain amount of stillness or about whom there is a certain sense of completeness, so that they do not need much attention. There is a certain tuning in that allows many things to be done without a single word being uttered. In many ways, they have made themselves a part of me. Even when they are around, due to minimal movement within them, I am still in solitude. The tuning in allows them to function in perfect harmony without the need for instruction and explanation.

"You are offering your place and your hospitality. I regret that I won't be around too much to enjoy it. I will be spending most of my time alone, but I will do my best to spend the evenings with both of you."

His comments only increased the mysterious quality of the week. Not knowing what to say, I simply sat in the silence, allowing it to permeate me. We remained silent for the rest of the short time until we arrived at the house. As we pulled into the driveway, I glanced at the clock on the dashboard. We had arrived fully forty-five minutes earlier than I anticipated.

As Sadhguru stopped the car and turned off the engine, the Rumi anthology that someone had given him at the airport fell off the dashboard. As I picked up the book, I could sense a charge to the stillness, a sense of expectancy in the quiet. Perhaps the fall of the book reminded him of my question back at the baggage claim—of whether love is the ultimate that one can seek—because softly, Sadhguru asked me, "Cheryl, are you looking for love or are you looking for the ultimate?"

For a moment I was taken aback. Since he didn't answer my question, when I asked it in the airport, I assumed he had not even heard it, but here we were, miles and hours later, and as if there was no time lapse he just picked up right where it left off. I pondered his question for a moment and said, "Sadhguru, I don't understand what the ultimate is. I understand what love is. All I know is that if there is more to life than this, then I want more."

He nodded. "Oh, there is more," he said. "There is much, much more."

CHAPTER FOUR
Night One: Midnight with a Mystic

*"Love is your quality. Love is not what you do.
Love is what you are."*
—Sadhguru

Just as we were getting out of the car, I noticed the headlights from Leela's Toyota minivan illuminating my driveway. Who says yogis don't have good timing?

Although Leela is only in her late twenties, there is something ageless and wise about her. She is a beautiful woman with long, jet-black hair, sparkling black eyes, and gorgeous skin. She seems to care nothing about the things most young women are caught up in. I often noticed that she wore exceptionally loose fitting clothes; when I asked her about it, she replied in her typically off-handed way that she preferred comfort to fashion. When I once commented to Sadhguru that Leela seemed to be totally indifferent to how beautiful a woman she is, he laughed and said, "People do not know how beautiful they are, so they need constant confirmation from the outside. It is good for her that she has lost such a need."

There have been many times when Leela's innate logic made me question just what I had been thinking. She has a very dry, crisp, often funny way of saying what is on her mind. She is certainly not afraid to speak out about what she is thinking.

When I first started doing a little volunteer work at Isha, I found myself working with some people that I did not particularly like. I thought they were flakes and that they were making things more difficult, confusing, or a lot less fun than they needed to be. From the time I opened my own business, I had spoiled myself by mostly only working with people I liked, respected, and thought were fun. When I carped to Leela that I was not used to working with or even being around people like this, she simply asked, "Old person or new person?"

"What does that mean?" I asked.

Calmly she explained herself. "Are they new to Isha or have they been around Sadhguru for a while?" I thought that was an interesting distinction. I could already see real changes in myself in the short time I had been a student of Sadhguru's. As I considered that, I began to see that many of the people I did not like were all quite new to Isha; and likewise the people who impressed me the most had been around Sadhguru for quite some time.

As I thought about it, I realized that even in the short time I had known them, I could see for myself the changes that were occurring in the people at Isha. I had once heard it said not to judge the Buddha by the Buddhists, but when I saw how some people were when I met them and how they were after coming out of so many things, I thought that it does reflect well on Sadhguru and the yogic technology he is teaching. Once I heard Sadhguru say he did not care how someone was when they came to him because, as he put it, "after being here, they will definitely change. No matter how they come, if they are willing, they will become beautiful beings here." In this context I had also heard Sadhguru once say that a good gardener will not complain about the condition of the soil nor about the poor seed, but will instead see how best to make it flower. It is in this that the gardener's skill comes into play.

Leela told me that when she first started volunteering at Isha Foundation, she would find the people she liked the least and work with them.

"Why?" I asked.

She replied, "I was interested in getting rid of all my boundaries, and they showed me where my limitations were."

That was a totally different approach from the way I had been living for the last thirty years. Funny, even though I considered myself a student of human potential, it never occurred to me that those boundaries make us smaller human beings. I used to protect my comfort zone so much. Leela has on several occasions said to me that a little discomfort is good.

Leela has a wonderful sense of humor, and we are constantly laughing when we are together. Still, I do not know how she keeps up with Sadhguru. His pace is absolutely super human. I cannot imagine how any human could keep the schedule that he keeps. If anything is an example of what having no boundaries might look like, it is all that Sadhguru is able to pack into his life. He hops around the globe easier than most people get across town.

I once took a road trip with them in India, with Sadhguru driving (of course). The gas pedal stayed on the floor and the speedometer stayed above 120 kph. When I asked Sadhguru if he thought we were getting too close to an oncoming truck, he told me he had "four inches."

Whew, I thought, now that's a relief!

Twice during that trip he stopped for *sathsangs* (spiritual meetings) in two different towns, where more than a few thousand people came to see him. He sat perfectly still and spoke for nearly two hours. Then we were back in the car and flying down the road again. The entire day was like this: fast driving punctuated by total serenity and presence while in the *sathsangs*. Finally, we arrived at our destination—at two in the morning. Four hours later, he was up playing soccer.

He maintains that pace day after day, year after year. As much as my energy level has improved after practicing Isha Yoga, Sadhguru's pace is unimaginable to me. After just a few days with him (let alone an entire week) and following his schedule of at most three or four hours of sleep a night, I am completely sleep deprived and have trouble putting words together to form a coherent sentence. But Leela goes nonstop with him for weeks on end with no apparent problem at all and very little sleep.

After we arrived at my house, Leela and I unpacked the car. Sadhguru disappeared into the room where he would be staying. His room, like the rest of the house, featured rustic furniture, wood paneling, and Native American Indian blankets hanging on the walls. A fireplace in the living room added to the feeling of cozy warmth and casual comfort. I lit a fire while Leela set about to make the kitchen her own for the week. Within a few hours, just before midnight, she served what would be the first of a week of incredible South Indian feasts—

without relying on recipes and rarely making a dish the same way twice.

Sadhguru joined us for dinner, and we settled in anticipating a long night of exhilaration and intrigue.

I put on a pot of water to make tea. Just as the kettle began to whistle, Sadhguru asked, "Tell me, Cheryl, do you still have that boat of yours?" I could see by the way the light danced in his eyes that he was ready to go out on it just then. I smiled. Never mind that he had been traveling for more than a day, a nighttime boat ride seemed to be exactly what he wanted. Though I'd had the boat for several years, never once did it occur to me to take it out in the dark, much less for a midnight ride. His eagerness to go again made me marvel at his high level of physical energy.

Midnight is normally my bedtime, but that night Sadhguru's unusual request gave me my own energy boost. I sprang up and led him and Leela through the sliding glass doors, down the trail, and onto the dock. "Ready and waiting," I bragged, thankful that the boat was gassed up and outfitted.

Then it occurred to me that I had left a few important things behind—such as the keys to the boat! I sprinted back up to the house, where in addition to the keys, I also grabbed a few blankets, a big flashlight, matches, and a pair of night-vision goggles.

The night was delicious, a perfect North Carolina summer evening: a pleasant temperature because of the elevation, warm but cooler than the summer days. As I emerged from the cabin with my hands full, I took a moment to notice and appreciate just how nice the outside air felt, and just how many stars filled the clear dark sky. The crickets and cicadas made a droning symphony, and the air was full of the soul-nurturing scents of the lake and soil and mountain forest.

By the time I returned to the pier, Sadhguru had already positioned himself at the helm. Leela and I sat up front as he backed the boat away from its dock, and off we went across the deep indigo darkness of Lake Glenview at midnight. Much the way he handled my car, Sadhguru handled the boat as if he was familiar with it. Water gently lapped the sleek, silvery pontoons that kept us afloat and stable as Sadhguru's smile seemed to actually brighten up the deep, night beyond. With a thrill of enjoyment, I noticed that we were the only people on the water.

It was perfect.

A short time later we came to a small uninhabited island. Sadhguru skillfully steered the boat to a sandy area with a fallen tree that we used as a makeshift dock along the wooded shore. As Leela and I tied off the boat, he went ahead of us to a clearing, where he promptly lit a roaring fire. We joined him and sat around the blaze, basking in the warmth and in its light that shone like a lone beacon in the midst of a vast world of darkness. A few minutes of silence passed by and then Sadhguru began chanting a vibrant, deeply haunting mantra. There is something so stirring when he chants that it is almost hypnotizing.

Nadha Bramha Vishwaswaroopa
Nadha Hi Sakala Jeevaroopa
Nadha Hi Karma Nadha Hi Dharma

Nadha Hi Bandhana Nadha Hi Mukthi
Nadha Hi Shankara Nadha Hi Shakti
Nadham Nadham Sarvam Nadham
Nadham Nadham Nadham Nadham

His voice faded into the greater silence that seemed to envelope us all, and we three sat in a noiseless, blissful peace for some time before I asked Sadhguru to explain what that beautiful chant meant.

"Loosely translated," he said, "this is what it means: 'Sound is Brahman, the manifestation of the universe. Sound manifests itself in the form of all life, sound is bondage, sound is the means for liberation, sound is that which binds, sound is that which liberates, sound is the bestower of all, sound is the power behind everything, sound is everything.'"

I thought about what that could mean and I remembered that there were also places in the Bible that also talked about "the word" and its overarching significance: "In the beginning was the word and the word was with God and the word was God." I thought that there is a great circle of connectedness between all the different spiritual traditions.

As the time melted away, Leela began to speak to Sadhguru about a young couple that had requested Sadhguru to marry them. When there was a lull in their conversation, I asked Sadhguru whether there was such a thing as soul-mates. I did not think there was, but the question was on my mind because of a discussion I had earlier in the week with my son about whether a perfect person exists for everyone. When I married at nineteen, I really believed that everyone had a soul-mate, and at that time I was convinced I had found mine, but after I was divorced, I quickly abandoned that idea. Even so, some of my friends, even at my age, were still looking for their perfect matches. I wondered if such an ideal situation could really exist. Perhaps, given my earlier failed marriage, I had just become a cynic about it all, even though I later bounced back from my divorce with a truly happy second life partnership. As appreciative as I am of the man in my life, I never burdened our relationship with the expectation that we had to be soul-mates for each other.

Sadhguru asked, "Are you asking if there is a soul-mate for everyone?"

"Yes," I replied, "that's my question."

"Now, you must understand this," Sadhguru explained, his eyes alive and bright as the reflection of the fire danced across his face. "Mating is always of the body. It's a body requirement. Maybe it is also of the mind and the emotions. So, the process of mating belongs to the body to some extent and to the mind to some extent. The soul cannot mate with anything, nor does the soul need a mate, because it is absolute and boundless. Only what is limited needs a mate in order to feel a little better."

This line of thinking, though logical, sounded quite stark and not the least bit romantic or fun.

"Why do you choose a mate?" he asked.

"I guess to find fulfillment," I answered.

"You want your body to feel a little better," he said with a smile. "We call that sexuality, and it can be quite beautiful. We want our mind to feel a little better. We call that companionship. We want our emotions to feel better, and we call that love. Emotional compatibility makes it very beautiful and sweet, but that is as far as it goes. Experiencing a good physical compatibility, companionship, and a strong sense of love in many ways can make your life very wonderful, but if you are willing to look at all this very carefully and sincerely, you cannot deny the limitations with which it exists and the anxiety that naturally follows such an arrangement. Though it is quite a fortune for a human being to find someone who is physically, mentally, and emotionally compatible, the limitedness of that arrangement invariably becomes suffocating if you are unwilling to settle for the limited.

"To have such a pleasant arrangement is like living in a beautiful garden. Every human being wants to have this, but this is not a matter of soul.

"All the connections you make this way are either of the body, mind, or emotions. You cannot connect anything else this way. Maybe if you rise in your awareness and attain a certain mastery over your energies, you can connect your energies.

"It is extremely important that we understand the limitations with which we are living and try to make the best of them for now, and then see how we can go beyond our limitations tomorrow.

"If you do not understand the limitations of your relationship, it gets greatly decorated, but when it crashes, it becomes so ugly you cannot even walk out of it gracefully. It becomes ugly simply because you tell many lies to yourself and to the other person.

"It is better to be straight, at least with yourself—even if your partner lacks the necessary maturity for you to be 100 percent straight with him. At least to yourself you must be straight. It is very important. If you want to live sensibly and joyfully, it is extremely important that you do not fool yourself. It is all right to fool the other person. You already know he is a fool because he has provided sufficient proof of that, as he has come to you," he said and burst into laughter.

"Thanks a lot," I said and also laughed even though I found his humor funnier or more charming when it was directed toward anyone other than me.

"Only if you are straight with yourself will you know the value of offering that to another human being. So, it does not matter," he said. "With him, you do whatever you think is the best. My business is not what you are doing with somebody else. What you do with someone else is just social. My business is just with you, basic you. With yourself, you must be straight.

"It is very, very important to be straight with yourself; otherwise, life won't work right. And if you are very straight with yourself, you will see through things very easily. There are lots of things that people think are important that won't matter to you or even make much sense to you.

"The more sincere you are with yourself, the clearer you will see things and the less melodrama you will add to things in order to make your life more intense and interesting. Without all the melodrama, you will become freer and freer, and you will quickly become less entangled. You will cut away one encumbering rope at a time. Then you will rise higher and higher to elevated realities.

"If you do not become absolutely straight with yourself, it may take a lifetime to deal with every little thing that disturbs you before you finally come to the point where you realize that all your worry was not getting you anywhere. You will need a full lifetime. That is a waste of your time—and life.

"But if you are very straight with yourself, you will see that most of the things that are highly romanticized in the world actually mean nothing. Actually mean nothing. They are all very empty. Life is full as it is. It does not need decorating. Only those who are missing the intensity of the life process—those who are not in perception of the grandeur of life within—have this juvenile idea that they have to enhance life. The life process does not need any assistance from you to become beautiful—if only you are willing to merge with it and know its beauty," he said and picked up a branch to reposition a couple of the logs in the fire. He also then added another large log, and the fire was soon a large, roaring blaze again.

He continued, "Does this mean you should not enjoy the simple aspects of life? No. Let's apply it to this moment. If you eat your dinner, will you get enlightened? No, but that does not mean we won't eat dinner; we eat. Why can't we enjoy the simple process of life? We will eat because we are hungry. Even though dinner is not going to get us to the ultimate, we still enjoy our dinner. Our bodies are hungry. Similarly, if you are hungry in your emotions, your body, and your mind for certain things, you get married. But you know very well that this is not the ultimate. This is a good way and a sensible way to handle your marriage. If you believe too many fancy things about it, then it cannot help but disappoint you. One day, it is definitely going to crash in on you. Even if you are married to the most wonderful person in the world, it will still crash because you cannot fool yourself forever. These arrangements are made to make our life journey pleasant for ourselves, also for those around us. What you call peace, joy, and love are all different levels of pleasantness."

"Sadhguru, do you think that some people should cut out marriage altogether if they don't think that it is right for them?" I asked.

"Why not? If there is no such need in you, you don't get into it. If you are not hungry, you don't eat dinner. You don't eat dinner because everybody else is eating dinner. The same goes for everything else in your life. If there is a need in you, you do certain things. If there is no need in you, you don't have to do it just because everybody is doing it."

As he spoke, I wondered how much I still allowed others to influence me. At this point in my life, I was pretty confident that I was definitely straight with myself, but you never know in what insidious ways you are influenced by the opinions of others. I have a vivid memory of when I became straight with myself. One cold, rainy night shortly after my divorce, my car had left me stranded on a busy road after work. It was three o'clock in the morning, and I was on my way to pick up Chris from the babysitter's house. While walking to find a phone booth in the pouring rain and thinking I did not really have anyone to call, I really grasped the starkness of being completely alone. For a time I had isolated myself from both my family and my friends. As I started to sink deeply into self-pity, something in me said, "Well you came into this life alone and you will leave alone; what you do with the middle is really up to you." As I absorbed this aloneness, I realized that I felt very close to the edge of life. I no longer felt that I had the insulation of a family or even close friends. I realized that the insulation I had felt before was only a false sense of security anyway. In reality, anything could happen to anybody, family or no family, friends or no friends.

Somehow this caused me to become friends with myself. Before that, I was much more influenced by other people. What that act of making friends with myself meant to me was that I suddenly got extremely honest with myself. It was a defining moment for me, and from that point on, I tried to tell myself the unvarnished truth. One thing I've discovered since doing Sadhguru's Isha Yoga is that you start to see yourself much more clearly. More of what you are doing comes into your awareness. Many things, like self-centeredness, are embarrassing to see. The clearer you see yourself and the less drama you add to your life the more your personal needs begin to evaporate. Embarrassing or not, as you begin to change with awareness, it is all absolutely worthwhile and essential.

As these thoughts danced through my mind, I glanced at my watch. I was surprised when I saw it was already 2:20 a.m. Time seemed to be flying as we sat together on our private island around the warm, glowing fire.

As Sadhguru talked, we each helped to keep the fire burning. I became deeply aware of my surroundings: the slight breeze that danced across our faces, the smells of the lake and the fire, positively delicious in their earthly familiarity. The fire was so warm and soothing as we sat on the island. I looked at Sadhguru and he seemed to know that we were not ready to leave. I ventured to ask another question.

"Sadhguru," I said, "I always thought that love was the ultimate, but you said there is more." I was referring to the conundrum he had posed for me earlier that evening. "What is this more? Is there such a thing as divine love?"

After a few moments he said, "Love is a human emotion. It is one of the most beautiful things a human being is capable of. Many cultures or so-called civilizations have suppressed love. Many people have made an enormous effort to export love to heaven. Love is of the earth, of the heart that is you. There has been too much talk about how love is God. You do not know whether God is love or not, but if you are willing, you can be love. Love is a human emotion. Human beings are capable of immense love. You do not need to go to heaven to know it. It is the tenderness of the heart that you call love. You know, even your dog is love.

"By teaching people that love comes from up above, we have made them more and more incapable of love. Love comes from within, not from above. If you free your mind of complex prejudices that you have developed by identifying yourself with one thing or the other, you will see that it is very natural and spontaneous for a human to be loving.

"The moment you divide the world into right and wrong, into what is yours and not yours, into God and Devil, your love becomes very conditional. It gets enslaved to the external situations and it will no more be your quality, but something that will only happen because someone else or something else is wonderful.

"To put it simply, as a human being experientially, you are just these four things: body, mind, emotion, and energy. Right now, the combination of these four is what you call 'myself.' The best the body can reach is health and pleasure. The best your mind can achieve is joyfulness and peace. The peak of your emotions is love. Your energies can reverberate either with a mundane feebleness or with a great intensity of ecstasy. These are the only realms of experience that are available to you as of now.

"Generally, people do not know much intensity of body, mind, and energy, but they are capable of intense emotions, whatever those may be—anger, hatred, jealousy, love, or compassion. For most people, emotion is the most intense part of them, and it dominates and decides the general quality of their lives. And, love is the sweetest of all emotions.

"If you ask someone whether they would like to be healthy or unhealthy in their body, or happy or unhappy in their mind, you know the obvious choice. Similarly, on the plane of your emotions, would you want to be loving or hateful or angry? If you are using your sense, you would naturally choose love.

"When I say the word 'love,' probably you think in terms of loving somebody, but love is not about someone else; it is your quality. Just as health is of the body and happiness is of the mind, love is your emotion. If the ones whom you love very much are not in your physical presence, you are still capable of loving them, aren't you? If the people you love cease to exist as you are sitting on this island, you can sit here and still continue to love them. Many people find the expression of their love only when someone is dead or about to die. We always love the dead, don't we?" He laughed before continuing.

"Every human being is capable of being absolutely loving, but each one has issues with almost everything and everybody around him. He has gotten into a mental state where no one in the world is okay except himself. The discriminatory dimension of his mind has gone berserk.

"Sincerely look at yourself and see. Look at the dearest person in your life and see how many layers of resistance to them you have. The moment your mind says that someone or something is not okay, you cannot love. You cannot love that which is not okay. As people make themselves more and more incapable of love with their judgments and opinions, the need for belonging forces them into a compulsive and destructive sense of attachment.

"Love is your quality. You are just using things and people around you as stimuli to find expression for this quality. If you bring sufficient awareness to the discriminatory intellect, loving is the only way you can be. Love is not what you do. Love is what you are.

"If you look at love as an emotion, see carefully what its objective is. When you say 'I love somebody' on an emotional plane, you are longing to become one with that person, so it is really oneness you are seeking. There is something within you that feels insufficient the way you are right now. Thus, you long to include another as a part of yourself. If this longing finds a physical expression, we call it sex. If it finds a mental expression, it gets labeled as ambition or greed. When it finds an emotional expression, you call it love or compassion.

"Love is just life longing for itself. This longing is a longing to become all-inclusive. To become all-inclusive is to become boundless. But, these attempts toward boundlessness and all-inclusiveness through physical, mental, and emotional means will remain always just a longing. Many times love makes you feel that you have reached boundlessness, but you always fall back to realize it was not so.

"If one transcends the discriminatory intellect," he said, "then you attain a state of *samadhi*. *Sama* means equanimity; *dhi* means intellect. It is a state of boundlessness and ecstasy that is beyond the limitations of body, mind, and emotions. Whether you go after sex, money, or love, boundlessness is what you are looking for. When a large part of you is still unconscious, the longing remains and you do not find the fulfillment, the ultimate. If boundlessness is what you are looking for, why not approach it directly?"

I listened in silence, but a silence in which my mind continued to work. I thought, So if boundlessness is what we really want behind every other desire and longing, what is the proper vehicle? Looking at Sadhguru sitting there in utter stillness, I wondered if he was the vehicle that could take us to the beyond. Without looking at me he said, "With these many questions on your mind, you cannot piggyback a ride." He added, "Let's say that while riding in the pontoon boat, we want to go to the moon. If we attempt it in that boat, we will not go anywhere. You will either crash upon the bank or dive into the water, mistaking a reflection for the real. To go to the moon you need an appropriate vehicle. Trying to reach boundlessness through physical realities amounts to the same: going to the moon in a pontoon boat."

As the evening wound down, the silence seemed to grow deeper within me. My mind kept returning to that haunting mantra Sadhguru had chanted, and as I thought of it, the fire, the evening, the peace, the quiet, and the companionship all let me slip naturally and easily into meditation. In that meditative state, I felt alive and at home, perhaps more so than ever before. It was an incredible experience of just being: pure, objectless consciousness that is timeless, without space, and indescribably joyful. This larger presence seemed to expand from deep inside me.

"Sadhguru," I said, "that mantra you chanted tonight is so stirring. Where did it come from? Is it ancient?"

"The stirring is not just a mantra. The mantra is just a medium. Actually, it is not ancient," he said. "It came to me when I was in the Himalayas, but that is a long story."

"Will you tell us the story?" I asked, so he began.

"Above Kedar, where you trekked last year, is a place called Kanti Sarovar. Generally, people do not go there. It is a very tricky climb. Several years ago I trekked up there and just sat on a rock. Anyway, for your information, this is the site of the first yoga program on the planet. The legend says that forty thousand years ago Shiva, the first yogi and the first guru of the yoga tradition, expounded the system of yoga in its full glory, depth, and dimension to the seven sages, who are revered in India as the Saptha Rishis.

"It is very difficult to put this into words, but after some time while I was just sitting there, everything in my experience turned into sound. My body, the mountain, the lake in front of me, everything became sound. It took on the sound form. You know, modern science has now proved that the whole of existence is just vibration. Do you know this?

"Quantum theory now says there is no matter, just the vibration of energy. Wherever there is vibration, there is bound to be sound. The question always comes that if it is sound, why can't I hear it? You cannot hear it because your hearing is limited to a small band of frequencies.

"The frequencies that are above your hearing are known as the ultrasonic frequencies, and the frequencies that are below your hearing are known as subsonic frequencies. What a transistor does is convert a frequency you cannot hear into one you can hear. So, we already know that there is much we cannot hear and that the whole of existence is sound.

"While I was sitting there above Kedar, everything became the sound form and was just going on in me in a completely different way. Even though I have a deep appreciation of Sanskrit, I never bothered to learn it because my own vision had never failed me and I did not want to read the ancient texts written in Sanskrit and clutter myself with all the traditional whatever. So here I am, sitting with my mouth closed—I am very clear about that—but my own voice is going on loudly, as if it is on a microphone, loudly singing a song, and it is in the Sanskrit language, and I am the song.

"That song was the one I chanted, the Nadha Brahma."

The three of us sat enveloped in a warm deep silence before Sadhguru smiled and said, "Cheryl, we are going to have to continue this tomorrow evening. The night is slipping away."

I did not want to leave, but I could not prolong our time on the island any longer. I looked at my watch in amazement; it was already almost four o'clock in the morning. A mere four hours had passed since we first ventured into the dark and got on the boat to come to this island. And yet, over the course of those four hours, I knew that I had been very near the ultimate, where the world takes on forms we do not know. As we prepared to leave, I thought, everything is so much stranger than I ever imagined.

And yet, it was about to get stranger still. . . .

CHAPTER FIVE
Night Two: Divine Bliss

"All that you desire either for things or people or power is a thirst to include everything as a part of yourself. It is your longing for boundlessness, your infinite nature."
—Sadhguru

I awoke the following day still invigorated by our conversation on the island and eager for our next one to begin. But true to his word, Sadhguru stayed behind closed doors in his own quarters. Since during the day he needed only the fruit and water we left in his room, Leela and I decided to hike nearby Whiteside Mountain, which is part of the Appalachian mountain system.

Formed 950 million years ago, the Appalachians rose higher than twenty thousand feet above sea level in some places in prehistoric times, but the range underwent widespread, prolonged cycles of erosion, and today its peaks are considerably lower. Whiteside, said to be one of the oldest mountains on the planet, is now one of the higher peaks in the southern Appalachians at a mere 4,930 feet.

As we began our hike, I thought of Sadhguru's love of mountains and his deep relationship to them. What he was doing during the day must have been pretty important for him to miss this gorgeous day. I was glad he told me he would get in at least one hike with us before we left North Carolina at the end of the week.

With water and snacks in our backpacks, we were ready to go in no time, and we felt carefree as we walked into the bright sunshine of a southern highlands morning. Overhead, the sky was brilliant blue and dotted with puffy, white cloud columns that reached from high in the atmosphere to very near the ground, so near you felt you could touch them. Soon we reached the nearby point where the trail begins its ascent up the slope, and we entered a shaded corridor that cut through young trees, their trunks spindly with the effort of sending their heads up into the light. At their feet sprouted some of Earth's most luxurious vegetation. Wild mountain flowers bloomed among masses of green moss, azaleas, feathery ferns, and stands of polished rhododendron.

Farther on, we saw large oaks, spruce, and hemlock trees with great limbs that canopied the trail and formed high, commodious nooks and crannies. We walked by rock walls hacked out when the trail was built, some of them wet from water seeping its way to creeks that eventually emptied into the Cullasaja River. After we had trekked for a while, we reached the summit, where the view opened up and we could see the hazy, tree-softened Great Smoky Mountains spread before us. Forty percent of the area is undisturbed national forest, and there is so much variation in elevation that many waterfalls gush and glisten down the slopes.

All this beauty was the reason I had chosen to have a cabin on the magnificent Highlands Cashiers Plateau, one of the prettiest places I have seen anywhere in the world. I planned to make sure Sadhguru hiked this trail at least once.

Leela and I found a secluded place to sit and talk, and the day flew by. I was very curious about many things I had seen happening to people at Sadhguru's advanced programs, and I was also interested in knowing more about Leela—why she was here and how she had changed since meeting Sadhguru. Unlike most people, Leela does not talk about herself easily. She did tell me that she had been around Sadhguru for sixteen years and that she had come to be with him because she wanted to be completely free of all limitations. But mostly, we talked about the intense experiences I had seen people undergo in Sadhguru's presence. Leela said she thought that the speed of one's transformation had to do with how open and willing one is to transform in the presence of the guru. Between the two of us, we planned to discuss this and several other topics with Sadhguru later that evening.

We were back at the cabin by mid-afternoon, tired but happy. Later, as night fell, we worked together in the kitchen, exchanging jokes and enjoying warm times as we prepared a fitting meal. I helped with the salad, while she did the gourmet cooking. She prepared a South India feast of *masala dosa* (mashed potatoes and traditional Indian spices), *sambar* (yellow lentils and vegetables), rice, cauliflower pickles, a delicious spicy cabbage dish, and a rice pudding.

With the cooking done and the dinner laid out, we awaited Sadhguru's arrival. It was about 10:20 p.m. when he walked down the stairs to join us, and with him came the soothing quietness and astounding sense of intensity he exudes, which never fails to send a jolt through me.

After dinner I sped through washing the dishes and then, like a troop leader, hustled my visitors out into the cool night air. Since this locale is a rain forest, the weather here changes as quickly as it does in the tropics. We had enjoyed the warm sun and a brilliant blue sky during the day, but that night a foggy mist rose like a curtain from the lake, and overhead, clouds obscured the moon and stars. We were hard pressed to find our way to the island and did so only with the help of the dim headlight on the

boat, Sadhguru's memory, and a large flashlight I brought
along.

Sadhguru was as undeterred by the fog as he had been
by any other difficulty I had seen him encounter, and
again he drove the boat at full speed over the lake. This
time, I was of two minds about his passion for speed. I
was apprehensive about the low visibility, but settled by
the cool assurance with which he handled the boat. I was
glad we would quickly reach our destination and be ready
to talk again.

When we laid anchor at the island, Leela and I helped
Sadhguru gather wood, and he began to build a fire as we
unloaded the blankets, flashlight, tortilla chips, and salsa
I had brought with us. By the time we were through,
Sadhguru had a roaring blaze that sent sparks into the
inky night, and he was sitting cross-legged before it.
Seeing him there, a sense of *déjà vu* came over me. We
were here again as if we never had left, inside the circle
made by the glowing fire, listening to the owls call and
the water patiently lap against the boat, and sitting in the
presence of a being so compelling it seemed to me his
imprint would forever remain on this little plot of earth.
How good it was to be here with him!

As we sat for a moment in silence, I thought about
last night's conversation and the guru's short discussion
of *samadhi*. In fact, thoughts of *samadhi* had been on my
mind all day. I knew it meant a state of bliss, but I also

knew the meaning was more complicated than what that short definition implied. I had many questions. I still did not understand its qualities, or more to the point, how one came to it. It seemed that the word "*samadhi*" was used to describe many different states of being. Were the people I had seen at the advanced programs experiencing it? Did it lead to enlightenment? Was it a taste of enlightenment, or was it enlightenment itself? Was it a temporary merging with God, or was it permanent? When Jesus said, "The kingdom of heaven is within you," was he speaking of this bliss?

"Sadhguru," I said, "will you talk to us some more about *samadhi*? I still have many questions. Besides what I have read, I saw a grave in India on which was written the word 'Samadhi.' What does that mean? Do you have to die to reach a state of *samadhi*?" I asked, half in jest, because I knew it was said that he was in a perpetual *samadhi*, or bliss state.

Sadhguru laughed out loud. He is a man of quick wit and easy laughter, and he enjoys subtlety. "Most people only experience peace and transcendence when they are dead," he said. "You know, in America you say, 'Rest in peace,' even as whole lives go by in restlessness. Have you heard of that woman who made a tombstone for her husband with an inscription, 'Rest in peace until we meet again'?" He asked while still laughing. "Resting in peace, unfortunately, comes for most people only in death.

"*Samadhi* means a state in which one has transcended the limitations of the body and mind, and this must happen in life and not in death. So, for those who are in a state of samadhi, there is no such thing as death. Death belongs to the realm of the body.

"Your body is just something you accumulated. It is a piece of earth you imbibed through food. This is just a piece of earth," he said, tapping his chest, "prancing around like this. Your body is on loan from the planet. All the countless numbers of people who have lived on this planet before you and me have all become topsoil, and so will you. This planet will collect back atom by atom what it has loaned to you. No interest, though," he said, winking.

"If one is constantly, experientially aware that both the body and the mind are accumulations one has gathered, then that is *samadhi*. You are in the body, but you are not it. You are of the mind, but you are not it. That means you are absolutely free of suffering because whatever suffering you have known enters you either through the body or through the mind. Once your awareness is keen enough to create a space between these two accumulations and who you really are—this is the end of all suffering.

"The root of ignorance is in being identified with the accumulations you call the body and mind. Your clarity of vision is cluttered with all your identifications and your personality. It is because of this limited identification that the distinct lines between what is me and what is you have been drawn. All disharmony, conflict, and suffering are rooted in this. *Samadhi* is a state where you have obliterated these distinctions, and you are looking beyond the wall.

"*Samadhi* can be a step toward enlightenment, but it is not essentially so. Staying in these states certainly hastens one's realization of boundlessness by setting up a clear space between what is you and what is not you. However, one can know and enjoy these states but still not know the essential nature of existence or become liberated from all the compulsive aspects of life."

"I've wondered about the people I see at the Isha programs who appear be to sitting in ecstasy for hours, tears streaming down their faces. Are these people in a *samadhi* state?"

"Yes, what you are witnessing in the advanced programs are various levels of *samadhi*. *Samadhi* is a certain state of equanimity, where the intellect goes beyond its normal function of discrimination. Once the intellect is on hold, the boundary of what is you and what is not you collapses.

"The very nature, purpose, and energy of a guru is to dismantle and dissolve the limitations. In my presence, you will always feel the insignificance of your physical and psychological needs because my very energy is tuned toward alienating you from them or creating a distance between you and your mind and body. Everything I do or say is aimed toward that. Once you allow my energy to seep into you, you will be in a *samadhi* state. How far you go depends on how far you are willing to allow yourself to go. All the talking I do is just to coax you to allow me to enter between you and your body-mind.

"Many people enter ecstatic states the moment I walk into the place where they are, even if they have their eyes closed, or even if they are mentally unaware of my physical presence."

I had seen that for myself. Many of my friends get so ecstatically intoxicated that for certain periods of time they have to be helped around like little children or have to be supported as if they are inebriated, but so blissfully inebriated that something in me longed to experience and know what they were going through. It was difficult for me to realize and accept that this did not happen to me not because of my balance or stability, but because of my insecurity and fear of losing control. I was not comfortable with the absolute abandon with which Sadhguru and some others at Isha sing, dance, and above all, live every moment of their lives. Sadhguru made it clear to me that what I think is control is actually suppression.

"But, one can know and enjoy these states and still not know the essential nature of existence or become liberated. You may meditate for twelve years and then come out of it, and even then you may not be a realized being, although you may be a little closer. When you go into another reality and stay there for long hours or years, the grip of this present reality is broken for you and you have an experiential understanding that present reality is not all there is. That's the whole purpose of long meditations.

"These states are not unique to yogis. Mystics and saints from all traditions have experienced and spoken about these things. One of the Christian saints, Saint John of the Cross, spoke of the necessity to go beyond all the boundaries one has known. Form, he said, must yield to the formless in order for the soul to be fully emptied."

Later I looked for Saint John's words. The quote reads this way: "Even visions of the holy Christ crucified, of God in resplendent majesty, or of the heavenly effulgence must be released in order to reach divine union."

"In Isha Yoga," Sadhguru said, "we have created powerfully consecrated spaces, where experiencing a *samadhi* state comes about very naturally. These *samadhis* are very pleasant, blissful, and ecstatic. There are also *samadhis* that are beyond this.

"Once you are liberated from all that you think is you, you will know the blissfulness of creation and creator. This blissfulness is the basis for you to experience dimensions beyond the physical, and it is the basis of true love and compassion.

"One who is concerned about the possibility of his own suffering can never know true love and compassion. Only when you are no longer concerned about yourself can you truly love."

"But Sadhguru," I said, "isn't love about giving and taking?"

He shook his head gently. "Love is neither giving nor taking. It is your longing to include the other as part of yourself. Giving and taking are arrangements you make for the fulfillment of the needs you have within you. Needs are of many kinds: physical, mental, emotional, social, and financial. Fulfilling these needs is a part of your survival process, but this is not love.

"Have I told you the story of the pretty woman in the park?" He asked with a smile. He is not one to hide his delight at the prospect of sharing mischievous, often biting, stories that usually make a point with equal parts brutal impact and compassionate clarity. I indicated that I had not heard the story, and he began. "One afternoon," he said, "it happened that Shankaran Pillai went to the park. When he arrived, there was a pretty woman sitting on a bench. Shankaran Pillai settled down on the same bench, and after a few minutes he moved a little closer to the woman. She moved a little farther away from him, and again he moved a little closer. She moved farther, he moved closer, and she pushed him away. He got down on his knees and said, 'I love you. I love you like I've never loved anybody in my life.'

"You know, women are sometimes fools for love, and things happened between them. At seven forty-five in the evening, however, he said, 'I have to go home!' She said, 'What? You are leaving me? You said you love me!' Shankaran Pillai replied, 'Yes, but my wife is waiting at home!'"

Sadhguru laughed (I did not think that particular joke was that funny) and then he got to the point. "Now, this 'I love you' has become a kind of mantra, an open sesame," he said. "You can get what you want just by using those words. What is really meant instead of 'I love you' is 'I have some needs I want to fulfill.'

"Of course, everyone does have needs they want ful-filled. There is nothing wrong about it and nothing right about it. If you see this clearly, then there is a possibility you can grow into your love. What is important is that you are sincere and truthful with yourself about it. In truth, only when you have the other's well-being upper-most in your mind do you have a taste of love. Otherwise, all you have is a mutual-benefits scheme. In this situation, if your needs are not filled, your so-called love will go away.

"Falling in love where your personality goes away is a way of dissolving your limited self or your person, and it can become a doorway to the beyond.

"You earlier asked if there is such a thing as divine love. Love is always divine. When you are touched by love, you are still here, but you do not belong here.

"However, if you are asking whether God loves you, you know many people are proclaiming that God loves them. The way they have made themselves, only God can love them. People are making themselves in a way that only God can love. Making yourself in a way that people cannot help but love you is significant. Being in a state where only God can love you is a pathetic way to exist, isn't it?" He asked and laughed.

"Jesus told you to 'love thy neighbor.' Loving your neighbor does not mean falling in love with the man or woman next door. 'Neighbor' means whoever is next to you right now, irrespective of who they are or what they are. Loving this way means that love is your quality. It has nothing to do with the other person. This love is given as freely and naturally as a flower exudes its fragrance. How can you love one and hate another when the same divine exists in all?"

"So, is love the way to merge into oneness?" I asked.

"The instruments for merging into one's ultimate union are many. Love is one way to get there. With intensity of emotion, one can get there. With razor-sharp awareness, one can get there. The very breath is a union with existence. There are many possibilities. One can also come to this by doing the yoga practices you are doing now. Generally, we are talking about using love as an instrument because it is a pleasant way of doing things. At the same time, you need to understand that in the process of love, you may get so entangled that you may not go any further at all.

"Now, when some people declare that love is God, they may be content and not want to go any further. They just want to remain in that little bit of pleasantness. I want you to understand this. You are not seeking sex, or love, or ambition—although these things allow you to experience a little bit of blissfulness. So, love is just a currency for your blissfulness."

He looked at me with his head tilted and his eyes shining, waiting for my next inevitable question. I watched the flames dancing over the wood for a moment before I spoke again.

"So, are you saying that love is definitely something different from bliss?" I asked.

"Cheryl, please understand this. The reason that you want to love somebody is because it gives you some sense of blissfulness. But, you will not be able to be blissful all the time. Sometimes you will be blissful, but sometimes you will still be anxious and miserable. Sometimes you will be frustrated. So, love is not bliss. Love may lead to certain moments of blissfulness. Sex may lead to certain moments of blissfulness. Fulfillment of ambition may lead to certain moments of blissfulness. All these are just instruments that allow you to become temporarily blissful. Once you become truly blissful, all the previous peak experiences of your life, like sex, or drugs, or whatever, will look like absolute kids stuff. I want you to be totally ecstatic and drunk on the inside like I am."

I remembered reading about Ramakrishna Paramahamsa saying, "Oh you boys, chasing after woman and gold when every pore of my body is orgasmic." I figured Sadhguru was saying the same thing.

"If you are blissful, will you seek sex or love? The answer is you will do what is needed and appropriate. It is not that you will be incapable of sex, or love, or ambition. All these things you will be capable of. It is just that you are chasing them because you do not know how to bring forth the blissfulness, which is the very basis of who you are. You are choosing roundabout ways to get there.

"What you call sex, love, ambition, or greed is just life's longing for itself. All you are longing for is to have a larger slice of life. Everything you are doing in your life is just this. It is life's longing to include and know itself in its totality.

"Whether you are aware of it or not, you believe that if you become just a little bit more, you will feel settled. The moment a little more happens, you long for a little more and a little more. Your thirst is not a longing for things, or people, or power. Your thirst is your longing for boundlessness, your infinite nature.

"Do you see that there is something in you that does not like boundaries? Even though this instinct for self-preservation in you continually fixes or creates boundaries, you still not do like boundaries. There is something within you that wants to go beyond the boundaries, to have and know a larger slice of life. How large a slice of life would settle you for good?" he asked.

"Nothing has ever settled me for good, no matter how wonderful my life might be at any given time," I answered.

"Even if I were to make you queen of the planet— don't worry, I won't make such a mistake—wouldn't you definitely look to the stars for more?"

I could see out of the corner of my eye that Leela found the image of me as a queen a really funny one, and I looked at her and grinned. Sadhguru, however, went on as if he didn't notice.

"Please examine this. Is your desire really for money, or just expansion? Hmm? It may be seeking money, pleasure, property, love, this, that, or whatever. But, fundamentally, it is seeking expansion. Whatever you achieve to satiate your desire, it is not working. Your desire is asking for the next thing and the next thing.

"Now, if you are aware that desire is only a seeking for expansion, how much do you want to expand? How much will do? You want to become unlimited. Desire is a spiritual process, but it is finding an unconscious expression.

"The very moment your unbounded nature got trapped in your limited body, desire was born. It is only because of desire that a spiritual process can be initiated because there is a desire to become unbounded. If this desire to become unbounded is finding unconscious expression, we call this a materialistic way of life. If the same desire is finding a conscious expression, then we say the spiritual process is underway. Both are the same. One is happening with eyes closed and the other with eyes open. You have to walk a path. So, shall you walk it with eyes closed or eyes open? Those are the only choices. Even if you walk with your eyes open, there are many pitfalls, but if you walk with your eyes closed, there is almost no chance of finding your way.

"You are seeking unbounded expansion. Seek it consciously. If you seek it unconsciously, your life will go to waste as you do many stupid things that won't mean anything to you toward the end.

"Seeking expansion consciously does not restrict you from doing anything. See, what you do, what kind of clothes you wear, and what you eat have nothing to do with your spirituality. Whether you are walking through your life consciously is what matters. It's not what you are doing. It's about with what level of awareness you perform an activity.

"My wish and my blessing is that you will walk with your eyes open in your life."

That is also my wish for me, I thought. I was so grateful that Sadhguru showed up in my life. It was difficult to believe I had only known him such a short time and that so much had already changed. As I was listening to Sadhguru, I heard a breeze stir through the trees. Looking up, I saw that the clouds had thickened, and it looked like it could rain at any minute.

"Now, when I say 'inner engineering,'" Sadhguru continued, "I am talking about just bringing forth the basic blissfulness in you, giving it expression. The reason it has not found expression is that your physical body, your mental body, and your energy body are not properly aligned. If these three are properly aligned, the inner blissfulness will naturally find expression. Once it permeates every cell in your body, you are no longer sexual, loving, or ambitious. You are capable of all these things, but your existence is beyond this. You are still part of the world, but you are touched by the divine, which will leave you in exalted states of exuberance. It is this exuberance you are seeking through money, power, sex, love, God— whatever may be your currency. All that you are seeking is to heighten the experience of your life to its ultimate possibility."

In the silence that followed his words, I thought about the vast sea of humanity of which I am part and how we are constantly looking for something, striving toward something, failing again and again and trying over again and again. I was beginning to understand that all this longing is only an unconscious expression of life trying to find its way to its natural peak. I became keenly aware of the crackling of the fire. It seemed to me that the wood was burning away like the fancy ideas I'd had. I knew that I really understood very little. In fact, the more time I spent with Sadhguru, the more I realized how little I knew about anything that really matters. I could see how most of us cling to our thoughts, opinions, ideas, and emotions because we have no perception of the real truth about life and love. Even though all my life I had thought of myself as a seeker of truth, I had failed to grasp even the simplest realities of my own existence. In my attempt to settle my discomfort, I had been living with many incorrect, fixed conclusions about things that were immensely important to me, but that were still out of my experience and understanding.

As I thought about my own perceptions juxtaposed with Sadhguru's penetration of the most profound aspects of life and death, I was compelled to ask him how he attained his clarity of vision. I wanted to know how he got to where he is now. After some time, I asked him to tell me the story of his present lifetime and how he got enlightened. Although I had read parts of the story, I longed to hear it from him.

He began, speaking as if he were talking about something that had occurred just yesterday. I was not surprised. I and others have marveled at his vivid memory, noticing in particular the thousands of people whose names and life details he easily recalls. "I never really was a child in my life," he began. "When I look back, I can clearly remember all the things that happened around me. I even remember situations that occurred during my infancy. I remember vividly who was in a room, what the room looked like, what was said, and what someone was wearing. My mother used to be stunned when I would describe in detail events and conversations I witnessed when I was three to six months old. Even as a child I was thinking the same way I do now."

Sadhguru said that as a youngster he had been called "Jaggi," short for his birth name, "Jagadish." Many years later he took the name we know him by now. He was a taciturn and yet quite joyful child, he said. Also, he was fiercely independent. He disliked being coddled and walked alone very early, even as his older brother was still being carried in someone's arms. He always seemed much older and wiser than his years and his friends and family members often came to him with their problems. Even his mother would confide in him, and then, realizing what she was doing, would ask, "Why am I telling you all this? You are only a boy."

Indeed, young Jaggi's loving, perceptive mother was often surprised and conflicted by the boy's words and actions. One such reaction occurred when he was about eleven years old. On this occasion, which he vividly remembers, something prompted his mother to express herself to him in a tender way. This rarely happened in those days, he said, since most Indian mothers were so completely devoted to their children that their love was obvious. Finding words for their love was rare.

After she spoke to him in this way, he responded with what seemed to him a simple, perfectly logical question. "If I had been born in the house next door," he asked, "would you still feel this same way about me?" She was taken aback. Tears filled his mother's eyes, and she walked away. The inquiry that seemed harmless to him was hurtful to her.

Half an hour later, his mother returned to him, still in tears. Silently, she touched his feet and then went away again. Jaggi realized that he had hurt her, but in his precociousness, he knew, too, that she was trying to come to terms with the truth behind his question. He knew very well that if he had been born into the house next door, she would not feel the same way about him. He knew this caused her to struggle inside herself not only over her love for her children, but also for her husband, her father, her mother, her everything.

The only member of his family he never surprised, he said, was his grandmother, who sometimes "danced in ecstasy" in his presence. Many of the family members considered her weird or crazy, but he did not think she was crazy. He loved her deeply and was drawn to her. She would sing and dance and cry and throw flowers with her feet at the gods—an absolute sacrilege, but she did it joyfully and lovingly. When he asked what she was doing, she would say, "Someday you will know!" His grandmother lived to be 113.

Not surprisingly, Jaggi was so full of questions that he found it almost impossible to sit quietly in his classes at school. He knew, too, that the teachers were only doing their jobs and, therefore, talking about things that meant nothing to them in their real lives. As a result, he skipped school as often as possible to go on hikes and treks. In spite of his absences from school, however, examinations were not difficult for Jaggi. He could quickly and easily read books and learn all that was needed to pass a test.

After the age of about ten, Jaggi often trekked to the place that eventually would become the scene of his enlightenment. It was called Chamundi Hill, located in the beautiful town of Mysore, where he was born and where his family lived much of the time while he was growing up. For him and his friends, this hill served as a racetrack where they rode motorcycles and a place to have parties. Later he even held business meetings there. But sometimes when he trekked alone, he chose to go into other, heavily forested areas. Here he would stay several days, eating the food he brought with him—a few loaves of bread and eggs he had boiled in secrecy.

He did not ask permission to go trekking because he knew it would not be given, but he always left his parents a note telling them when he would return, and he always returned on the day he said he would. When he disappeared into the forest, he would spend the days walking and sitting in the treetops, swaying with the breeze. After some time in the trees, he would become ecstatic, blissful, but he never realized until he was much older that on these occasions he was meditating. Years later, he would begin to teach other people to meditate by swaying.

Often he would return home with a bagful of snakes he caught in the forest. He was profoundly fascinated by the creatures, loved to catch them, and he was very good at catching them. (When he was a grown man, he realized that this fascination with serpents had survived in him from hundreds of years in the past.)

Jaggi was seen as a very different sort of boy from most, vibrant but very quiet and of few words. When he did speak, people sat up and paid attention. He was also quite wild. His parents were frantic when he disappeared, and once he came home, they repeatedly reprimanded him for his behavior. Predictably, they were also disturbed by his bagful of snakes. The sole redeeming aspect of the boy's adventures was that he always returned exactly when he said he would.

Jaggi's parents tried hard to keep him from acquiring the five or ten rupees he needed to purchase bread and eggs for his treks, but he always found a way. His father all but despaired. He had no idea what to do with his strange son. Often he lamented with his head in his hands, "What will happen to this boy? What can we do with him? He has no fear at all in his heart."

Jaggi's lack of interest in formal education continued as he grew older. "I passed my pre-university courses," Sadhguru said, "because I could just read a book and get what I needed to know, but then I announced that I was not going to go to college. My father was a prominent physician, and he wanted me also to become a doctor. My family did everything it could to persuade me to attend college, but I refused, saying, 'I will educate myself.'

"Despite all the protests from my family, I did not enroll. Instead, I spent most of that year in the library. Mornings, before the library doors were open, I would be there. All day until the library closed, I would be there. I got so involved; for one whole year I never even bothered to have lunch. I learned more academically that year than I ever would have learned if I had enrolled. I just read everything from physics to philosophy, geography to history, literature to *Popular Mechanics* magazine. During that year, I enjoyed and became very interested in English literature.

"Everyone had been so angry with me for not going to college that when the next academic year commenced, I let my mother cajole me into going to the university. My parents again tried to persuade me to major in medicine, or at the very least engineering, but I refused. I decided that if I went back to college, it would be for English literature. They asked me what I was going to do with such a degree—read poetry all day? I was not concerned, as I never had any intention of capitalizing on my education."

Predictably, Jaggi did not sit docilely in the literature classes. Finding that his teachers read from prepared notes, he simply requested that they let the students photocopy the lecture notes so that they would not waste precious time and energy in classes and the professors would not waste time and energy reading their notes out loud. His professors were not amused, but because of his high grades, they let him go to college in this unorthodox manner for the rest of his college years. His attendance would no longer be required.

"So I planted myself in the college garden," he said, "and people started coming to me to share their problems. I was surprised that everyone had so many problems. I did not choose this; it just happened." He was, in effect, holding court in the university. Even though he never had any problems of his own, he was sympathetic to what others considered problems.

When the time came for Jaggi to graduate, he wrote fifteen papers at one time—and received high marks for them. Encouraged by this show of academic excellence, his father wanted his son to pursue a master's degree. Jaggi refused, saying that enough was enough, and besides, he had already read everything on the master's degree syllabus. His long-suffering parents at last gave up trying to influence their son's educational choices, and Jaggi set out to make enough money during the next two years to travel, which was the time it would have taken to complete the advanced degree program.

"I always loved to travel and explore without having any planned destination. It was only the border checkpoints that limited my travels," he said. "I had already crisscrossed India on my motorcycle, and I thought I would ride all over the world."

Sometime after Jaggi's twenty-fifth birthday, his destiny began to unfold on his beloved Chamundi Hill in a very unexpected way.

He went there one afternoon and at about three o'clock, he parked his motorcycle and sat down on a big rock that had a stunted purple berry tree growing in its crevice. His eyes were open as he sat there, but something began to happen to him. Suddenly he did not know what was him was and what was not him. "All my life I had thought, this is me," he said, pointing at himself. "But now the air I was breathing, the rock on which I was sitting, the atmosphere around me—everything had become me.

"The more I say about this, the crazier it will sound because what was happening is indescribable. What was me had become so enormous, it was everywhere.

"I thought this lasted a few minutes, but when I came to my normal senses, it was about seven thirty in the evening. My eyes were open, the sun had set, and the sky was dark. I was fully aware, but what I had considered to be myself until that moment had just disappeared.

"Here I was, sitting on a rock, and the tears were flowing to the point where my shirt was wet. I was wildly ecstatic, although I did not know what was happening to me. When I applied my logical mind, the only thing it could tell me was that I was losing my balance. That was all my mind could tell me. I did not know anything about spiritual experiences. I had not been brought up in any kind of spiritual traditions. I had been fed with European philosophy: Dostoevsky, Camus, Kafka, and the like.

"Of course, I grew up in the sixties, in the time of the Beatles and blue jeans. Those were the things I knew, and here I was, exploding into something completely beyond my ability to grasp. I didn't know what it was, but it was so beautiful I didn't want to lose it."

About six days after this incident on Chamundi Hill, Sadhguru said, he experienced timelessness again. He was sitting at the dinner table with his family for what he thought was a minute or two, but in reality he was there seven hours, fully aware, though his old familiar self was not there. Everything else was there.

This timeless, bodiless phenomenon happened again and again with more and more frequency, and each time it happened, he neither slept nor ate for many days. One stretch was thirteen days. He did not know what this was; he did not have a name for it.

Then people began to say, "Oh, he is in *samadhi*," and they put garlands around his neck and touched his feet. Some wanted to know things such as what the future held for them or when their daughters would be married. He had no words to describe all this.

Everything about him began to change. The way he perceived and experienced life changed dramatically. Even his physical body changed—the shape of his eyes, the timbre of his voice, his body structure. The changes were so dynamic that the people around him could clearly see he was undergoing some kind of major transformation. After about eight weeks, the *samadhi* state became an enduring reality. Then he continually saw everyone and everything as part of himself.

After knowing and experiencing the ecstatic state of all-inclusiveness that had become continuous in him, witnessing other people going about unrealized in painfully limiting ways even though they had the same possibility within them, brought him constantly to tears of compassion. These tears of compassion slowly evolved into a resolve to strive beyond all personal limitations and comfort in offering this possibility to as many people as possible. It is an expression of this resolve and compassion that led to the creation of innumerable powerful methods to lead people into higher states of experience and aware-ness, which Sadhguru innovatively called Inner Engineering.

Later, he said, as he became seasoned to this blessed state, he was better able to handle his compassion, but in the beginning it was difficult to be steady. The energy had to be expressed. The unbounded had entered him and he could not hide it. It is no small matter when the divine descends upon you.

By this time in his life, Jaggi had built a few highly successful businesses, but when he began experiencing this blissful state, it also empowered him with a deep insight into people's minds, and he felt he had an unfair advantage over everyone around him. He decided to walk away from all the businesses he had painstakingly built from nothing. He began to travel, and soon lifetimes' worth of memories from the distant past began to descend on him.

"The skeptic that I was did not want to believe any-thing about previous lives," he said. "I was not the kind to believe anything of that kind. I was not somebody who would even enter a temple. I was not somebody who believed anything I could not see and understand. I fol-lowed up on all the memories that came to me. I went to the places I recalled from previous lifetimes. I met people and did much skeptical analysis of all the revelations that were coming to me. What I was remembering was clearer than daylight, but my logical mind would not accept it. I had to go through the whole process of verifying it.

"From that time on, a certain vision for creating an energy form that is of immense possibilities, an expression of the compassion of my guru from lifetimes past, became the single pointed agenda of my life. The making of this energy form involved complex inner processes and such unbelievable twists and turns on the outside. People who were witness to it know most of what happened. It is too much of a fairy tale for anyone else to believe. I would not believe it if someone told me about it. That is all I can say about it."

Sadhguru's vibrant voice fell silent, and I felt as if the space around us was pregnant with an intense force beyond my comprehension. It was overwhelming. When I was in India, I meditated inside the shrine that houses this energy form called the Dhyanalinga: a large cylindrical structure encased in a seventy-six-foot dome building made of burnt bricks, mud mortar, and other traditional materials. I wanted to know more about this mysterious structure, in which I had experienced such profound peace.

After sitting in deep solitude for some time, I found my voice and asked him what was uppermost on my mind. "But Sadhguru," I said, "why did all this happen to you? Why were you chosen for enlightenment, and why did the making of the Dhyanalinga become the agenda of your life?"

He nodded playfully at me. "If you really want to know the answer to that question," he said, looking at his watch and then the dying fire, "we will have to take this story back several lifetimes. . . ."

As if to punctuate his thought, thick, fat raindrops landed mid-fire, sizzling and bursting like overcooked marshmallows. Sadhguru smiled radiantly as Leela and I got up and scampered away for the pontoon boat. He followed us and then gently stilled my hand as I reached for the padded key chain still stuffed in the ignition.

"Look out over the lake," he said. Beside the rain, the fog was so thick we could not see a foot in front of us. There was a sheet—make that a wall—of impenetrable precipitation. "How will you navigate through that? Let us sleep on the boat rather than fight to get back to the dock and sleep inside your house."

I opened my mouth to protest, but he silenced me with a smile. "Tomorrow the sun will rise and we can get home quickly. Tonight, why worry about it? You thought to bring blankets, and the roof above your boat is all the shelter we need. Rest, and tomorrow we'll return home at first light."

In case I haven't told you, I can be very determined. I know the lake well, and I thought I could get us home, so I had to make the attempt. But after thirty or forty minutes of trying to navigate in the hopelessly blinding fog, I gave up. Sadhguru was right. There was no way to get home. I could either keep us awake the rest of the night looking for the house, or we could get at least a little sleep on the boat.

We turned off the engine, and Leela and I curled up under a blanket like my two miniature Dachshunds. Sadhguru lay on his back and went straight to sleep.

And so, as my second midnight with the mystic crept toward a wet, soggy dawn, I fell asleep wondering why in the world I still resisted what he said about even simple things.

Leela woke me at first light. The boat had bumped into the shore, and she wanted to make sure it was okay. I checked. Everything was fine. We both got up and looked around. We had only slept a couple of hours, and the fog was still impenetrable.

As we surveyed the situation, we looked at Sadhguru, who was still sleeping peacefully on his back in the same position he had fallen asleep in. He had not moved an inch. As I looked at him, I said to Leela that we were not doing a very good job of taking care of him. She nodded her head and said, "I know. Don't tell anyone."

CHAPTER SIX
Night Three: "And Now, Yoga"

"We don't need more Hindus, more Christians, more Muslims;
we need more Buddhas, more Jesuses, more Krishnas—the
real ones. Live ones. That is when true change will happen.
And that potential is innate in every human being."
—Sadhguru

As Leela and I peered into the fog that still hung over the lake the next morning, we were both a little worse for the wear. As always, though, Sadhguru awakened completely rested and bursting with energy.

By now it was six fifteen. The sun was starting to rise, but the cloud cover was still so thick that we couldn't see as much as a foot in front of us. Far from alarming, it felt absolutely enchanting to be the only ones on the lake, enveloped by all that thick white fog. Stranded—no closer to home than we were to the fire-lit island we'd left behind hours earlier—but safely cocooned inside the mist, we were free to pick up where we left off. It was as if the previous night's storm had never even happened.

Remembering last night's question about how Sadhguru came to be the way he is, I decided I couldn't let it fade away, as I knew the mist would at any moment, so again I asked him how he had done it. How had he liberated himself, and what part had yoga played in all it.

As if expecting not to be let off the hook, Sadhguru replied, "Yoga first entered my life long before, even beyond this present body."

To some extent, I knew what he meant. I had heard some stories of his past lives, and he had earlier told me that his enlightenment in this lifetime was more a "remembrance" for him and that this was, in fact, his third enlightened lifetime. But of course, I wanted the entire story. What were those other lifetimes like and how did they fit into his now being a guru? So I kept prodding, and at last the strange tale unfolded.

As the guru began to speak, Leela and I were off again on our journey into his fascinating mystical world. I felt as if I was in some ancient place, and sitting smack in the middle of a swirling white fog bank didn't hurt. It was as if the setting were bending to match the story.

Two lifetimes ago, Sadhguru said, he had been an intense seeker of the ultimate nature. He left home when he was seventeen and became what is referred to as a wandering *sadhu*. He traveled all over southern India on foot, pursuing yoga in the Shiva tradition, and he became a yogi known as Shiva Yogi, named after the first teacher of yoga.

In his incarnation as Shiva Yogi, Sadhguru devoted his lifetime entirely to his liberation, pursuing the goal of enlightenment with intensity and great perseverance. His journey to liberation was not made in comfort. He went through heartbreaking spiritual disciplines and was often without food. As a result of his single-mindedness, he became quite accomplished as a yogi.

At this juncture, I asked Sadhguru to backtrack and tell us why he had been drawn to yoga when he was Shiva Yogi. I got what I asked for. Incredibly, he responded by taking the story quite a bit further back in time, almost four hundred years to the early 1600s, when he lived in Central India as a vibrant youth called Bilva.

Ever the questioner, I interrupted again to ask why all his lifetimes had taken place in India, and he replied rather cryptically that they hadn't. He said that just the last three were lived there, and that twelve lifetimes ago he lived in Africa. He said that only those last three life-times were spiritually significant. I was mulling over just how many lifetimes this ancient being may have lived in all as he continued the story.

Bilva, he said, was a fierce devotee, wild and intense, and possessed a certain clarity of vision that allowed him to look into the hearts of other people. One of Bilva's passions was snakes, and he was the snake charmer in an intuitive tribe at a time when snake-charmers were considered holy men influenced by the gods. They were magicians, healers, and soothsayers.

Tribes to this day still practice this art. On one of my visits to India, I was amazed to be witness to a tribal snake charmer outside of a temple area where many tourists abound and all kinds of people sell vegetables, clothes, crafts, and an assortment of other things. I was up the hill from him and glad to be a good distance away when I noticed a very strange event. This bare-chested, long-haired, intense-looking Indian man was sitting on a blanket and mumbling some unintelligible words and sounds. As he started tapping his feet slowly and deliberately upon the ground, slowly snakes from the wild began moving toward him. Within thirty minutes, there were a dozen snakes—including cobras—crawling toward him. He collected them in his bag. This was bizarre to see. The ability to charm or call snakes implies some sort of unknown supernatural knowledge.

During that lifetime, Bilva's understanding of snakes was one of the personal characteristics that propelled him toward greater spirituality. He was a defiant and rebellious young man in his twenties, and because one of his acts of rebellion angered certain people, his life was brought to an early end. He was tied to a tree and put to death with bites from a snake, a cobra. The poisonous venom of the cobra contains powerful digestive agents that quickly and painfully destroy tissue, producing massive hemorrhaging and bursting the anal cavity.

Bilva knew all about snakes and was aware of what was going to happen to him from the snake bite. As the venom ran through his body and he was very close to dying, he locked his anal cavity—in yogic language this is called Mooladhara Banda—and he began to focus on his breathing. Bilva did not choose consciously to invoke this yogic discipline of watching the incoming and outgoing of the breath, a spiritual discipline of Kriya Yoga called Ana Pana Sati Yoga. He began to watch his breath spontaneously because he was trying to die with as much dignity as possible and breathing was the only function left to him. The young man watched his breath even as he experienced excruciating pain, and as a result, he lived the last few minutes of his life in heightened intensity. When he died, he left his body in awareness.

Bilva's breath watching was a gift of grace, Sadhguru said. Because he died in awareness, a new spiritual process began, took root in his being, and changed him in many ways. His spiritual quest had begun. It continued in his next life and carried him to the path of yoga. He then became the yogi called Shiva Yogi.

Shiva Yogi went many places and tried many things, and he suffered much hunger and physical hardship. He became accomplished in the various arts and intricacies of yoga, yet for all that, the ultimate self-realization eluded him.

At this point in Sadhguru's story, I again questioned him, probing for specific details about the yoga he practiced as Shiva Yogi, since today he puts so much emphasis on yoga as a means of self-transformation. He replied that what he did then did not really matter because he did not attained *mukthi*, or complete freedom from bondage. However, through the mastery of certain aspects of Kriya Yoga, he did attain certain capabilities that eventually gave him the freedom to exist without food and water for long periods of time and to walk through seemingly solid material such as walls. Above all, he attained enhanced perception that allowed him to grasp the past, present, and future of any person. Still, because ultimate realization eluded him, he was left with a certain rancor and with a burning longing to know the ultimate.

As Sadhguru spoke of Bilva and Shiva Yogi, I was conscious of his deep stillness and of the swirling mist behind him. He looked like an ancient bronze statue, a figure of immense antiquity, whose eyes seemed to see far more than what existed in the moment we presently inhabited.

As I sat before Sadhguru in what seemed a deep pool of peace, my thoughts were about reincarnation. Instinctively, when I first heard about reincarnation from my first meditation teacher, it made much more sense to me than living only one lifetime. I've read a lot about it since, but my initial fascination with multiple lives eventually faded. The past was only relevant to me as a way to understand how I got here and to the extent I could learn from it. But now that I was stranded in the fog with an enlightened being who could remember his past lives, I wanted to understand how he was able to become such a profound mystic and what part his past played in it.

"Reincarnation is more an evolution than anything else," Sadhguru said, answering my question before I asked it. "Animals also are evolving, but once you have a human birth, you can take your evolution into your own hands.

"And now, yoga," he said. "You can hasten your own evolution with yoga. You can go from a limited being to one who is completely beyond all limitations. Yoga is not just about physical and mental well-being, even though they are easily handled with yoga. It is about breaking the limitations of this dimension and moving into a totally different sphere of life: from the physical world to another existence by itself. This other dimension is right here—it is not somewhere else—but it is not available when a person is rooted totally in their physical nature.

"If one is totally rooted in the physical nature, one identifies with limited things and feels insufficient. As a result, you begin to accumulate material things. It is the nature of the mind to accumulate. When the mind is gross, it wants to accumulate material things. When it becomes a little more evolved, it wants to accumulate knowledge. When our emotions become dominant, the mind wants to accumulate people. The mind is a gatherer, always wanting to gather something. When a person starts thinking or believing he is on a spiritual path, then the mind starts accumulating so-called spiritual wisdom. Maybe it starts gathering the guru's words. But whatever it gathers, until one goes beyond the need to accumulate, whether it is food or things or people or knowledge or wisdom, it does not matter what you accumulate; the need to accumulate means there is an insufficiency. This insufficiency, this feeling of being insufficient, has entered into this unbounded being only because somewhere you got identified with limited things that you are not.

"If one brings sufficient awareness, and above all, a constant *sadhana* (spiritual practice) into his or her life, the vessel slowly becomes totally empty. Awareness empties the vessel. *Sadhana* cleanses the vessel. When these two aspects are sustained for a sufficiently long period, then your vessel becomes empty. Only when this emptiness arises does grace descend upon you. Without grace nobody really gets anywhere. For you to experience grace you have to become empty; your vessel has to become totally empty.

"If you do not experience the grace, if you do not make yourself receptive to the grace, if you do not empty yourself in order to bear the grace, then the spiritual path is something that needs to be pursued for many, many lifetimes. But if you become empty enough for grace to descend, the ultimate nature is not far away. It is here to be experienced. It is here to be realized. It is going beyond all dimensions of existence into the exalted state. It is not tomorrow; not another lifetime. It becomes a living reality," he said.

While sitting there absorbed in thought, the fog began to lift and I could hear the morning chirping of birds. A great blue heron flapped its wings as it took off in flight, trumpeting its wild prehistoric shrill to announce the dawn of a new day. I was chilly and wrapped the blanket tightly around myself as I wondered how many lifetimes I would have to go through before I could become empty. I didn't want to keep going round and round like a child stuck on a carnival merry-go-round. I wanted enlightenment *this* time.

"Why do we have this desire to accumulate?" I asked him.

Sadhguru looked down at his hands and answered. "This whole attitude that wherever you go you must gather as much as you can has come into you long ago. One basic culprit for this has been your education. It has always taught you how to gather more and more things. You learned systematic methods of gathering. You can make a living this way, but no matter how much you gather of things, people, knowledge, power, or even so-called spiritual wisdom, they are incapable of liberating you. They are incapable of taking you one step closer to your ultimate nature. To bring the necessary awareness and to constantly cleanse your vessel requires *sadhana*, or inner work. This is yoga.

"The only other way to jump the line into liberation, if you do not want to go through the struggle of awareness, is to be so innocent you simply surrender. This is Bhakti Yoga. But thinking minds are not capable of this. Surrendering is not something you do. Surrendering is something that just happens when you are not. When you are absolutely willing and you have no will of your own and there is nothing in you that you call yourself then grace descends on you. When Jesus said, 'Come, follow me,' almost all who heeded his invitation were simple peasants and fishermen. The educated, sophisticated, and scholarly did not respond. And of course, Jesus made it clear that only children could enter his kingdom of God, which means that only the innocent and childlike could walk the path of devotion, faith, and surrender."

I thought with a certain sadness of how many of us have lost sight of that simple path of humility. Not everyone, of course. Still, it seemed that many religions veered far away from the teachings they were built upon.

Sadhguru stretched his arms wide as if taking in the whole morning. Then he said, "I would always stick to the path of awareness and *sadhana*. If you naturally jump the line and shift from awareness to devotion, that is wonderful; however, but cannot be cultivated. Cultivated devotion is not devotion, just deception."

"But how do we do it then?" I asked.

He continued, "The web of bondage is constantly being created only by the way we think and feel. Whatever we are calling 'awareness' is just a way to start creating a distance between all that you think and feel and yourself. What we are referring to as *sadhana* is a way to raise your energies so that you can tide over these limitations or these mechanisms with which you have entangled yourself in your thoughts and emotions."

I said, "I also heard you refer to the process of emptying as 'dissolving.' Can you explain what you mean by that?"

"Dissolving does not mean putting yourself in a barrel of sulfuric acid," he said with a grin. "The personality you unconsciously constructed was fundamentally dictated by the instinct of self-preservation. Your personality is a mask you wear to face the world, but this personality, or mask, in your experience has become you. You have become completely identified with it. If this mistaken identity, this you, is dissolved, bliss will be a natural state, as it is your essential nature. To face the world you can always make faces as the situation demands, but you need not be identified with the role you are playing."

I had many roles in my life: businesswoman, mother, companion, friend, and daughter. I tried to imagine myself without those various identities. It wasn't easy to separate "me" from all those personas, even though I have always had something in me observing my life from a very slight distance.

Looking around, I noticed a break in the fog and could see the thick stand of trees at the water's edge not far from where the boat was floating. It was a tangle of branches, leaves, and shrubs.

"Sadhguru," I said, "we talk about spiritual growth, yet if what we really want to do is just dissolve this separate identity, is 'growth' the correct word?"

"Growth is toward dissolution," he said. "As you dissolve the limited creation of your persona, built with a complex amalgamation of impressions that you have taken in unconsciously, the boundless source of creation begins to grow in you and becomes a living presence in your life. That is the dissolution we are talking about, the dissolving of the bondages that make you a limited existence. When we talk in terms of spiritual growth, it is only because a logical mind can never think in terms of dissolving.

"Another way to reach zero is to expand, expand, to infinitely expand. That is also zero. Zero and the infinite are the same. The path of expansion is a more suitable concept for the ego to identify with.

"If people tell you to just 'drop the ego,' it is not going to happen. Much as you try, it is not going to happen. So, instead of dropping your ego, expand your energies. Even saying, 'I have no ego' is a very egotistical statement. The ego is a shadowlike structure. It is the very first result of your identifying with your body. The moment you started kicking in your mother's womb, the ego was born.

"The ego is your shadow. It is not good or bad. External situations govern shadows. When the sun is not at its zenith, you have a shadow. So, the ego is not the problem. The problem is that you have lost the distinction between what is you and what is your ego. Trying to get rid of your ego is much like trying to get rid of your shadow. If you tried to outrun your shadow, you would only become exhausted and frustrated, but if you just turn around, the shadow would be behind you. The ego is much like this. It is there. There is no such thing as living without ego. It is there, but if you are aware, the ego will serve you.

"You expand unlimitedly until you dissolve. Growth means expansion, and at the same time growth means dissolution. Only in ignorance do you think they are different."

"So, what actually reincarnates?" I asked. "This separate identity? If we eventually merge into oneness with the divine, which is already our innermost core, there really isn't a separate soul, is there?"

"What is referred to as a soul actually is a fiction. In the context of rebirth, of going from one birth to another, you have to have some understanding of the mechanics of how you are built. When you say you are a human being, you usually mean your outermost periphery, your physical body. In yoga, we look at everything about us as separate bodies because it is easier to understand that way. So, we see the body as five dimensions, or five sheaths.

"The physical body is referred to as the food body. The second one is the mental body. The third one is called *prana*, or energy body. These three bodies—physical, mental, and energy—are all in the physical dimension. They are physical existence. The physical body is very gross, not subtle. The mental body is subtler. The energy body is even subtler, but all three are physical. You can look at a light bulb for an example of a similar relationship. The light bulb is physical. The electricity is also physical, and the very light that it emanates is also physical.

"The physical, mental, and energy bodies are physical dimensions of life. These three carry imprints of karma. Karma is imprinted on the body, the mind, and the energy, and the imprint, or structure, is what holds it all together. Karma is the cement that holds you to the physical body.

"The other two bodies are non-physical. One of them is like a transient state and the other is completely non-physical. The non-physical body is referred to as the bliss body. This bliss body inside you is 100 percent non-physical. It has no form of its own. Only if the energy body, mental body, and physical body are in shape can they hold the bliss body in shape. It is like an air bubble. A certain amount of air is held in a bubble. The moment you take away the structure, the air becomes one with everything else. If these things are taken away, the bliss body will become part of the cosmos. So, if the karmic structure is completely dismantled, there can be no soul left. Everything merges into everything else. If the karmic structure is dismantled 100 percent, you merge with all existence. This means there is no you."

As Leela and I sat huddled together on the boat, I could detect more of a break in the clouds and I could hear many more sounds of morning around the lake. People were starting to wake up and let out their dogs, and a few fish were jumping. I could also smell bacon cooking somewhere nearby.

Sadhguru continued, "This non-physical dimension—the very core of who you are, which we can refer to as no-thing or everything—is the basis of all creation. It is the ultimate intelligence that creates, maintains, and destroys all existence. This nothingness or this boundlessness is referred to as bliss body because that which is non-physical cannot be described, so it is only inferred in our experience. When one is in touch with this dimension beyond the physical, one will be drenched in blissfulness. So, when we say bliss body, we are referring to it in the context of our experience of it as being indescribable. When we say liberation, we mean becoming free of the very process of life and birth and death. Liberation means coming free from the karmic structure that holds these bodies together, becoming free of your very existence."

"Sadhguru," I said, "is this bliss body, or our inner self, actually God in a way? Is it that we can either be this little limited person or we can be God?"

"What you call your self is also the universal," he replied. "It is not different. It is just that now this peel, or covering," he said, stopping to indicate his own body, "has formed over the universal aspect of you. With yoga, you begin to differentiate the energy levels in yourself. You create a whole system. You create spiritual practices. The body and mind—the peeling—subside in importance, and the self stands out. Now you have a better chance of really looking at the self, experiencing it. This is the whole *sadhana*. Whatever you call yoga, the spiritual practices are just meant to reduce the importance of the body and mind and to bring out the importance of the self.

"Enlightenment is not something that happens. It is always there. The spiritual practices, or *sadhana*, that you do enable you to see that it is there. You are not doing *sadhana* to construct divinity within you. Many people in the United States talk about self-development. Self is one thing you cannot develop. You can develop the mind, which is fine. You can develop the ego, which everyone does anyway. How can you develop the self, which is absolute and boundless?

"And, if you could develop the self, you had better discard it because it would be incomplete stuff. Only that which is incomplete can be developed. If something is already all-pervading and eternal, how can you develop it? So, *sadhana* is not about building something. It is not about creating divinity within you or becoming enlightened. Divinity is already there within you. *Sadhana* is just a way of opening your eyes. *Sadhana* is like an alarm bell. The whole thing is just a process of waking you up, waking you up to another level of reality.

"There is no such thing as self-knowledge. There is just self. That is all. Jesus made this clear. He talked about himself and his father in heaven, but at one point he said, 'I and my father are one.' The you that is beyond all limitations and that which you are referring to as the almighty are the same," he said, looking deeply into my eyes as if to make sure I understood this. I knew there were people who would think this idea was sacrilege, but as he spoke, I also knew he was trying to impart a vital truth. I realized that most of our lives we live in a fog just like the one that still lingered over the dark waters of the lake.

"How can we experience this if we're trapped by these limitations?" I wanted to know.

"You must become willing to transcend your limitations. This willingness is surrender. The only barrier to it is you. If you are willing, who can stop you? So, the *sadhana* is just to make you willing. Enlightenment is never far away, but to make a person completely willing takes time because you have layers and layers of resistance. It takes time to work through the resistance, to become absolutely willing. It need not necessarily take time, but generally people do take time."

"Sadhguru," I said, "in this culture, saying that you could evolve into a god would offend many people I know. Yet, self-realization is something that is striven for in India. Can you tell me why there is so much difference?"

"India is a very ancient culture that has produced many enlightened beings," he said. "There are two kinds of cultures in the world. One culture is always waiting for God to come down as a human and transform the world. This is one kind of culture.

"The other kind of culture is saying that the only way to transform oneself and the situation is to turn into a god. Yoga comes from this culture. In yoga we have no incarnations of God. We see the possibility that even we can become like God, blissful and all-seeing.

"Whatever you hold as God, we can become, and everyone has the same opportunity to do so. If only one person is God, or the son of God, what are the rest of us? What are all of us? We also come from the same source. Only those who are totally prejudiced say, 'No, my God is different; your God is different.' Only then is there a problem. Don't forget that Jesus, after he was done with enticing people by promising to take them to the kingdom of God, turned around and said, 'The kingdom of God is within you.' He also said, 'You can become greater than me.'

"A Buddha or Krishna or Jesus is not looking for followers. They are striving to manifest the divine they know to be present in all beings.

"Anyone with a little sense can see that all life has definitely come from the same source. So, if we all come from the same source, all of us carry the same energy within us. Some people call it God, some people call it Allah, Einstein called it E, and we are calling it Ishwara or Isha.

"Whatever you call it, all of us carry it within us in an unconscious way. In fact, if you make it conscious and allow this energy to express itself, you also are the divine. That isn't to say that until then you are not the divine—right now you are also the divine, but unaware of it. Whatever you are unaware of does not exist for you; you must understand that. If you are sitting right here and an elephant is standing behind you, such a big animal, and you are unaware of it, it does not exist for you. Only when you become aware of it does it exist for you. Similarly, although God is within you, as long as you are unaware of your god-like nature, it doesn't exist for you. When someone becomes aware, he also becomes aware that everybody carries the same potential."

"Sadhguru," I began, "is every person capable of reaching the peak of their consciousness? Will this yoga really work for everyone, or just for special beings like you or for people who are intense seekers?"

"Yoga definitely works for everyone. Let this be clear. Yoga is a technology, so there is no question of it working for one person and not working for another. Your telephone, your television, your computer works for everyone—even though most people do not have a clue as to how they work. You just have to learn how to use them. Depending on their expertise, different people can use them at different levels. Most people will never understand how yoga works, but it definitely works for everyone. Factors such as age, attitude, or karmic situations, to name a few, decide how quickly yoga works, but it definitely works, whether you can immediately notice it or not. Some people will catch fire like gasoline, some will burn like paper, others will burn like wet wood, but yoga can definitely hasten everyone's evolution."

"Does this always take a long time, or can it happen quickly?" I asked. What I really wanted to know was how quickly this could possibly happen for me.

He said, "It could take hundreds or even millions of rebirths, or this transformation could happen in just this moment. If it is the one and only purpose of your life and all your energies are focused in this direction, it is not far away. The problem is that people have so many other priorities that spirituality is on the side. What you are seeking is within you. If it is the only priority of your life, nothing can stop you. If you are willing, what is within you cannot be denied to you even for a moment. If it was a question of capabilities, we could prescribe a certain amount of time. When you will become willing, tell me, who can decide?"

"But, Sadhguru, if that is the only priority in our lives, what happens to our lives as we know them?"

"Life as you know it is not a barrier. If realizing your ultimate nature is the only priority of your life, everything you do will naturally orient itself toward that. Your work, your relationships, your love, your money, your very life's breath will orient itself toward your ultimate nature. The experience of every little human thing you do becomes extremely fulfilling and joyful when it is done in the light of great purpose. Once your ultimate nature is your only priority, the life process, the little acts, the thoughts, and the emotions will become a joyful and fulfilling process."

I was relieved to hear this. The world is so full of distractions that it is difficult not to lose focus. I was very concerned that only those who walked out of their lives got enlightened, and even then, only very, very few. They say it takes everything you have and then some. Some people take this literally, and I am sure there is a lot to that, but even then there is no guarantee. You can still be identified with your body and mind. So, how do we come out of all we are identified with? Knowing my ultimate nature was a huge priority to me but I was still clueless as how to use everything in my life for transformation. So, how? How do I do everything in my life in the light of this great purpose of transformation?

I asked, "But, how does yoga actually lead to transformation?"

"Cheryl," he said patiently, "yoga leads the body to a state where it is perfectly in tune. When your mind, body, energy, and your inner nature—which is the seed of creation—are perfectly in tune, the best of your abilities will naturally flow out of you. Do you see that when you are happy, you have endless energy? Have you noticed this?"

"Definitely I've noticed that," I answered.

Nodding, he continued, "When you are happy, your energies always function better. Even if you don't eat or sleep, it doesn't matter. So, just a little bit of happiness liberates you from your normal limitations of energy and capability.

"Yoga is the science of activating your inner energies to such a vibrant and exuberant state that your body, mind, and emotions function at their highest peaks. When your body and mind function in a high state of relaxation and with a certain level of bliss, you can be released from the physical and mental problems many people suffer from. With the practice of yoga, your body and mind will be kept at their highest possible peaks, which naturally leads to a certain mastery and control over one's life and destiny."

This was definitely becoming true for me. I was functioning at a higher vibration or cruising at a higher altitude, so to speak, than I ever had before. Things that used to bother me no longer touched me. My happiness was no longer so dependent on external situations. In fact, to my own amazement, in some ways I was better able to mold the outside situations, including people whom I marked as difficult to cooperate with, and create what I wanted.

"You told me before that peace of mind is just the beginning," I said. "So, how exactly does yoga work to transcend all the limitations?"

"You can transcend the ropes that bind you one rope at a time, or you can explode out of your limitations. What you refer to as your capability is really a certain way your energy functions. As you gain mastery over your energies, you will do, simply and naturally, things you never imagined possible. Americans are enamored with technology, so I'll use the following analogy: Yoga is really just the technology of using your energy for higher possibilities. When one's inner energies are activated, one enters an altogether different sphere of perception, experience, capability, and possibility. In other words, you can grow to a point where everything that can ever be done within the laws of nature can become yours.

"Did you hear what Mark Twain said after his meetings with the Indian mystics?" Sadhguru asked.

"No. I love Mark Twain but I do not remember anything he said about India."

"He said, 'Anything that can ever be done by man or by God has been done in this land.'"

As if the elements were listening to Sadhguru, we now had a magical moment where the sun burst magnificently through the clouds. After we had soaked in the welcome warmth of sunshine for a few minutes, Sadhguru suggested that we head for the house. As immersed as I was in our conversation, I reluctantly agreed that it was time to go. The rest of the story would have to wait.

I could now recognize where we were. I pointed out the direction of my house, Sadhguru started the boat, and we headed across the lake. When we arrived, the guru went back to his room, and Leela and I decided to each take a short nap and then do some grocery shopping.

Again the day sped by, and that evening Sadhguru joined us much earlier than usual. Since there was still some daylight left, he suggested we take a walk. The area around my lake house is so beautiful, with breathtaking views stretching all the way down to the lake, that we decided just to walk there rather than waste the little daylight that remained driving to one of the hiking spots.

As we walked, I took the opportunity to ask Sadhguru about some mundane matters. One of my friends who knew that the guru was going to spend a week at the lake had asked me to try to get him to speak about money and about whether each person actually has a specific calling in life.

I hesitated before bringing up these topics. It seemed like a waste to take time with a spiritual being to talk about money and vocation—when he knows so much about things that are completely unknown to the rest of us. But, I reasoned, since Sadhguru deals with people as they are, and since for Westerners money is so important, perhaps it was legitimate to ask him. I had personally been all over the map about money, from thinking it did not matter at all because it did not make people happy to being worried about not having enough and then thinking it was so important that I spent way too much of my time acquiring it.

Once we had been walking for a few minutes, I posed a question. "Why," I asked, "does money seem to take such a toll on the lives of many people here in the United States? Many of the people I know are spending the majority of their time working for money and yet often feel they don't have enough money or, for that matter, enough free time thanks to working so hard at making more money."

Without hesitation, Sadhguru replied that people often ascribe too much value and too many qualities to money. He said that money is just a device to make our transactions easier. When I pressed for more, he said, "Money is a device that started with the barter system. It was not complicated. It was just a means of exchange, a tool to make life more comfortable. If money is in your pocket, life is more comfortable. Money is not the problem. The moment money enters into your head it becomes a perversion. You get identified by it. It becomes who you are. How much money you have becomes part of your identity. Once you get identified by it, you can never have enough.

"There are many wealthy people who become just miserable with even a little fluctuation in their net worth. But money is merely a means to an end. Like everything else, money has been created for our well-being. We forget this when we become deeply identified by it.

"Instead of just having money to use, we become someone—or something—because of it. Then we begin to compare ourselves to other people instead of enjoying what we have. This becomes a kind of a sickness, where making money is then turned against your own well-being. Everyone has different capabilities. If you just look at your own capabilities without comparing yourself to others, you will find a way to have enough money by doing work you enjoy without all the struggle. Money is definitely needed, but how much money do we really need? If we would change our idea of a successful life to a joyful life, we would find our need for money would dramatically decrease.

"How much money, how much comfort, does one actually need to live joyfully? Never before have people been as comfortable as they are today. The kinds of comforts and conveniences that even royalty did not have a hundred years ago are available to ordinary people. Yet, it cannot be said that we are happier than our ancestors. Once money becomes part of your identity, a certain fear and discomfort comes along with it, no matter how much money you might have. This is not an intelligent way to live. The very thing that was supposed to bring you comfort and the hope of living happily turns against you. We may succeed in creating outwardly perfect lives, but the true quality of our lives is based on our interiority."

"Sadhguru," I said, "why does it seem that yogis are against comfort?"

Sadhguru laughed and said that yogis are definitely not against comfort. "They want to be comfortable in every situation at all times, even lying on a bed of nails," he said. "They just don't want to settle for the small comforts that most people are after. Comfort is not dictated by external situations. True comfort arises with a certain level of ease within yourself.

"In today's world, we make economics the most important part of human life. Your love is not important, your joy is not important, your freedom is not important, your sensibilities are not important, your music and dance are not important. The most important thing is your economics. Today, in any city, if you say someone is a big man, it does not mean he is the most intelligent man. It does not mean he is the most loving man. It does not mean he is the most skillful man. Definitely it does not mean he is the most meditative man. It simply means he has the most money in town. So, our whole orientation has become economics. Unless the subtler aspects of life become important, we will not be joyful people. If you would stop comparing yourself to other people, you would find that your needs would come down drastically, and you would live much more sensibly—a sense that is most essential to save and sustain this planet, the very basis of our lives right now.

"Money is an empowerment, but by identifying yourself with it, you are making it an impediment. There is nothing wrong with money. If you leave it in your pocket and do not identify with it, it is useful. Once it gets into your head, it becomes a perversion. If you would make your inner well-being the top priority of your life, you would find that money is easily handled."

"Sadhguru," I said, "I know that your father was a physician. Did you have an affluent upbringing?"

"Money was not an issue in my home," he said. "My father had a very good career, but money was not a central focus. My father's father was a millionaire, but my father refused all the family wealth that was his for the asking. Instead of going into the family business, he became a physician. When my father was just five years of age, he lost his mother to tuberculosis. As she withered away in those days without the needed remedy, she wished that her son would become a doctor. That desire took root in him even though his father wanted him to take over the family business. One thing that stood out about my father was the way he always put other people first. Whether he was on call or not, he would immediately respond and act even for a minor issue whenever he was called. Money was never involved. I can remember many times when the family was sitting down to dinner and he would get a call to help someone. He would get up and go. My mother would ask that he at least take a minute to finish his meal, but he would always just go.

"Now in my grandfather's case (that is my mother's father), it was quite different. He was the richest man in the town. My grandfather was enamored with his money, but my grandmother was very spiritual. The contrast between the two made a big impression on me when I was young.

"Every day there was abundant cooking going on at my grandparents' house, and in the morning all the beggars in the town were fed there, three to four hundred of them. My grandfather ran his own kind of kingdom. He sat at the front door for his business affairs, starting at six thirty in the morning. The first thing was the feeding of the beggars, and those gifts to them were recorded. Maybe he believed they helped him to buy his tickets to Heaven. Then he got on to his financial transactions. He lent money to anybody and everybody in town, and people came in the morning to pay their interest, to settle their loans, or whatever. He also lent money to the class of people called the untouchables. To those people, he would just drop the money, as he did not want to touch them.

"While my grandfather ran his kingdom, my grandmother ran a different sort of kingdom out of the rear door. People came to my grandfather because they couldn't help it. He had the money, the power. After they finished with him, after they went through the terrible experience of dealing with him, many of the same people found their way to the rear of the house where my grandmother would sit. She had nothing to give, but everybody wanted to be there with her for at least a few minutes. The same people that my grandfather would not touch, my grandmother welcomed at the back door and enveloped in her love. They shared their lives and their problems with her.

"I was fascinated by this. You know, these two kingdoms at two ends of the house. Somehow I always felt my grandmother's kingdom had more grace and beauty about it, since people came there because they wanted to come. People went to see my grandfather because they had to go there: They had no other way. I am sure that if they had enough money, those same people would have had nothing to do with him.

"When my grandmother was sixty-four, she moved out of the house. Though the family owned large tracts of land in the area, she went and set up a little temple on someone else's land, and this was an absolute disgrace to the family. They were the richest people in the town, yet she built her small temple with her own hands on someone else's land, and she lived there off that person's land. She grew her own vegetables there.

"She would often come to my grandfather's house for three or four hours in the mornings, especially if we were there visiting. When we went there for vacations, she made sure to come and spend a few hours with us, and she used to do something in the morning that fascinated me so much. She would take a plateful of her breakfast and go outside with it. She went to where the squirrels, sparrows, and other creatures were, and little by little, she put out her food for them. She put it everywhere. At least three-fourths of her breakfast she put out for the little creatures before she ate anything, and she talked to them as if they understood her language. Sometimes she talked to them verbally, and other times she was just really sort of with them.

"Most of the family dismissed her as crazy, but what she was doing with these little creatures fascinated me because she was really with them. To me as a child, what she was doing looked quite natural. She was communicating with the animals just as one would speak and communicate with people.

"It was only much later that I thought about what she was doing. Many times she wouldn't eat any of her food at all. When someone was there, they would ask, 'Why aren't you eating?' 'I already ate,' she would say. 'I ate with the squirrels.' She fed them and she felt full herself. It was not an emotion. It was real to her. She really felt her stomach was full, and it was enough. She lived to be 113, so it must have been okay.

"So, much later, when I started experiencing things very much out of the ordinary, every little thing she did suddenly meant so much more to me. Before, I liked it, but I could not understand the depth of transaction she had with life."

As Sadhguru paused, I again questioned him. "You mentioned that one of your grandmothers would sing and dance in ecstasy and throw flowers with her feet to the gods," I said. "Is this the same grandmother?"

"That's her. How could there be two?" he replied, nodding. "Later on, so many more of her ways became clear to me and have become mine, too. All that she was means so much more to me now."

We walked a while in silence along the path and stopped on a promontory overlooking the lake that gleamed serenely in the sunlight. Around the edges, the reflections of trees created a perfect mirror image of the shore. But my mind could not be still like the lake. I wanted to get back to my other question, so I said, "Okay, another question. Do people actually have a life's calling?"

Sadhguru laughed. "If life is calling you," he said, "you must go toward it with utmost passion and involvement, not with hesitation and calculation. As survival happens to be a basis for life, only when it is taken care of will the finer and subtler aspects of life find a place in society. This is not about the ego problem of wanting to do something different; it is just about your living to your full potential. If you are truly passionate about every aspect of your life, you will realize very easily what you are good at. You may be good at *eppume illadadi.*"

"What is that?" I asked.

"That means you may be good at something that has never been done before, something completely new. But, even if you are not a complete original, even if you are doing the same simple, age-old things, when you do them with utmost passion and involvement, they will raise you to a new dimension of experience. Problems come when people are passionate about only one thing, or when they are passionate in an exclusive way. This often leads to isolation. Exclusive existence and a very limited involvement will only lead to frustration and pain. I am talking about all-inclusive passion.

"One must be in touch with everything one's five senses can perceive in a given moment, be absolutely passionately involved with that. This is true compassion. Compassion is not an attitude of kindness but an instrument of unprejudiced involvement.

"The way life happens is first being, then doing, and then having. But right now, because you are trapped in your mind, you are always thinking first of having. You come to a stage in your life when you want to have a certain kind of life that includes a certain kind of mate, house, car, or whatever. How to have this? Now you are thinking what to do. The moment you start thinking what to do, the people around you start advising you.

You start thinking doctor, lawyer, export business, or whatever. Once you do one of these professions for a period of time, you start thinking you have become something, and then you are just moving against life. You are going the having-doing-being way, and it leads to an endless pursuit of having, which is the basis of an unfulfilled life. You must first establish your way of being. Then, whether you get to have what you desire or not, you will still be wonderful. The quality of your life is decided by your way of being and what you get to have is only a question of capability and conducive situations. If you make this simple shift to being, to doing, to having, then a large part of your destiny will be by your will.

"Now, I want you to get this right: There is no *life's calling*, but life is calling—both from within and without. Only when you truly respond to the call of life will you know life in its entirety. Only when you know an unprejudiced and absolute involvement with the universe, every atom in the universe, will you explore, experience, and know the full scope of who you are. And, in this absolute involvement, you need not be limited by your own past experience and capabilities; you can imbibe and have access to the great storehouse of knowing that is the very nature of the universe. It is also through this absorbed, unadulterated involvement that one can know the true nature of the self, which is boundless, and the basis of all, which is the ultimate destiny that the all-desiring process is actually leading you on to."

A few flimsy white clouds scuttled by overhead. At this point, we were coming to the end of an inlet and would soon be headed back toward the lake house. Even though everything we talk to Sadhguru about ultimately comes back around to our knowing who we are, I still wanted to ask him about some more of our obstacles. "Sadhguru," I said, "many people in this country are so stressed out and it is ruining their lives. What can they do about it?"

"First of all," he said, "why are people becoming stressed? When I first came to the United States a few years ago, wherever I went, I noticed that people were talking about stress management. I could not understand that. Why would anybody want to manage their stress? You want to manage things that you value, don't you? Do you want to manage things you don't care for? I can understand that you want to manage your business, your property, your family, your money, things like that, but why stress?

"It took me a while to understand that people have come to the conclusion that there is no way to live without stress. Stress is an accepted part of life here. But the truth is that stress is not a part of life except when you have lost your sanity. Stress is not happening because your job is difficult. It is happening because you are incapable of handling your own systems. You don't know how to manage your body or your mind or your emotions or your energies. If you know that, then nothing is stressful because you are no longer hijacked by external situations."

In the silence that followed these words, I mulled over what he said. We had heard, I thought, an aspect of his teaching that reached down deep into the everyday experiences of living. I was glad I asked the questions I had thought might be too shallow.

As we continued to walk and chat, we came around a bend in the path and heard, and then saw, two dogs loudly and aggressively charging at us from a short distance away. Previously, I had had a close encounter with one of the dogs, a red chow whose reputation for being hostile and confrontational preceded him. His owner had been told more than once to contain this uncontrollable dog. In fact, some of the neighbors had called Animal Control several times about him, but the dog was pretty crafty and so far had not been picked up.

I knew this dog by sight, and he had been joined by another scary, rabid-looking dog. When I saw them charging at us, I screamed. Sadhguru motioned for Leela and me to stay back, and we stopped and waited as he walked on. To my surprise, when the ferociously growling dogs saw the guru coming, they immediately sat down meekly by the side of the road as if contained by some unseen force.

After Leela and I gingerly passed the dogs, I expressed my surprise about the way they were suddenly subdued. True to form, Sadhguru laughed and said, "I would not relish a piece of meat being pulled off my body, though they would! After this, these dogs may be a little more civilized, although their owners probably will not approve of their guard dogs becoming gentle creatures.

"Cheryl, I want you to understand that life around you will respond and create itself to match the way you are and not the way you or the people around you think you are. What you think about yourself is existentially irrelevant."

We walked on in silence after that, but no matter how serene my surroundings were my mind would simply not quiet itself. I could not get over how even aggressive animals seem to know who Sadhguru is. So many things happen when I am around him that I would normally find extraordinary, yet in his presence they seem perfectly normal.

This experience with the dogs reminded me of something that happened on the Himalayan trek I took with

Sadhguru and Leela. The trek began on a gorgeous September day, and I was among several hundred people trekking in the breathtakingly beautiful Himalayan Mountains of India with Sadhguru. I had read much about the Himalayas and the yogis and mystics who lived there, and for years I had wanted to visit those mythic mountains. When the opportunity arose to explore this incredible region with Sadhguru, I jumped at the chance even though less than fifteen months earlier, because of health conditions, I was not able to walk even a quarter mile.

On this extraordinary day, we were climbing toward mystical Kedarnath. It is fairly high up in the mountains, at more than twelve thousand feet in elevation. This was no ordinary trek; I knew that Sadhguru was particularly fond of Kedar. He spoke of it often with love and reverence. It is a place where many saints and sages have lived, and still do. It is said to be a captivating place of intensity, solace, wisdom, wonder, and wildness.

The day we walked to Kedar, the sky was brilliant blue and the sun shone the whole way up the mountain. It seemed a day made just for us. Although the air was warm at the base of the mountain, it got quite cold as we climbed higher. That day we trekked close to nine miles. Along our way, there were tea stalls where one could get chai, Limca (a lime drink), or Fanta orange sodas. One could also get bottled water and some crackers or cookies, and a few stalls offered cooked Indian food.

Each person in our group was walking at his or her own pace, so even though we were a large group, we walked mostly alone and in silence. As we made the ascent, we encountered many people not among our entourage who were walking or riding horses or mules up and down the mountain. Some were being carried by local people in a kind of basket. Apparently this mode of transportation was not uncommon at high elevations.

When I was about three-fourths of the way up the mountain, I came by chance upon a yogi and about twenty of his followers, who also were walking up toward Kedar. Their dress, demeanor, and symbols indicated that they were staunch worshipers of Shiva, who in the yogic culture is seen as an adi-yogi and adi-guru, the first yogi and the first teacher of yoga. As such, he is known as the greatest guru.

Legend has it that Shiva actually lived on pristine, glacier-fed Lake Kanthi Sarovar, which means "lake of grace," located about two miles above Kedar. He is said to have visited Kedar often to meet and instruct the yogis and sages there. For this reason, Kedar is considered his abode, a place that evokes his presence.

The yogi we encountered on the mountain wore a simple, unstitched, off- white garment and a shawl, and he had holy ash smeared between his eyebrows. He was barefooted and one of his shoulders was uncovered, but he did not seem to be bothered by the cold air. He was set apart by his intense, smoldering eyes, his beautiful face, his long, flowing black hair, the grace and agility of his stride, and the air of strength about him. He looked about fifty years old and appeared to be a guru himself. He was noticeably more self-assured than the people with him, even arrogant, and you could tell they looked up to him. His power was apparent.

I walked on and soon lost sight of the distinctive-looking guru, but I saw him again several hours later beside the river near the top of the mountain. He seemed to have no fatigue after the long trek.

Then I saw one of the Isha volunteers from our group approach him and start talking to him about Sadhguru and the Dhyanalinga, a meditation shrine that Sadhguru built in South India. The yogi said, "Why are you telling me this? I do not care about some guru or some shrine. You obviously cannot see who I am. I am Shiva!" The Isha volunteer was taken aback. This was like saying, "I am the ultimate" or, "I am God."

Despite his shock, however, the Isha volunteer was not dissuaded and continued to talk to him about Sadhguru. They had quite an animated discussion, with the yogi continuing vehemently to dismiss the talk and the volunteer and to loudly claim that he was Shiva. The meditator then said, "If you are Shiva, you should definitely meet my guru; he will be coming here soon." The other man shook his head in disagreement.

This heated exchange continued a little longer at an escalating pitch until the volunteer gave up and walked away. The yogi stayed there with his group. A short while later, I saw Sadhguru himself approaching, looking very stylish and decidedly unspiritual in trekking pants, hiking boots, an Indian-style shirt, and aviator sunglasses. In no way did he look the part of a yogi.

As I watched, the intense, barefooted Shiva caught sight of Sadhguru and something amazing happened. This yogi, who was so proud, who seemed to need no one but his own godly self, went running to Sadhguru and threw himself on the ground before him, flat on his face in full prostration.

Dogs, ordinary people, Native American elders, and even self-proclaimed Shivas all respond to Sadhguru in the most extraordinary ways. In spite of all that, he constantly downplays his importance and keeps himself as accessible to his students as possible to keep us from feeling overwhelmed and awed by him.

CHAPTER SEVEN
Night Four: Into the Mystic

"It is human aspiration to function at the peak of body, mind, and energy. Yoga is a technology that facilitates the fulfillment of that aspiration."
—Sadhguru

Our eventful late afternoon walk left me with simultaneous feelings of relief and hunger. Even Sadhguru, despite his tenacious will and relentless energy, appeared to be due for some nourishment. He and I sat on the porch, relaxed and refreshed by the cool, breezy mountain air, while Leela busied herself in the kitchen.

I glanced in at her from time to time. She had tied up her luxurious black hair, and while she worked, her face appeared bathed in the stream of remaining light that shone through the kitchen window. Seemingly without much effort, she assembled yet another magnificent feast, which we ate quietly. Inwardly, I continued to marvel at the way one gentle spice merges with the vibrancy of another to create layers of flavors, and I wondered how in a mere thirty minutes Leela could produce such a symphony of tastes, smells, and delights.

But Leela's gourmet cuisine was not all that was on my mind. As quickly as she could combine her ingredients to create a magnificent meal, so too our week together seemed to be passing at warp speed. Between the time spent in silence and reflection and the lightning bolts of illumination and clarity that energized our conversations with Sadhguru, the hours marched by relentlessly. Like the others before it, this day would also be gone in a flash. Even as I tried to savor every moment, as much as I wanted the minutes and hours to last longer, the time still passed at an unprecedented speed.

Midnight rolled around again, and so we went down to the boat and cast off, returning to the island and to the story of Sadhguru's life—or, in his case, lives—and to the importance of yoga in his (or anyone's) journey. As soon as we were all settled in our spots around the fire, I wasted no time initiating the conversation. "Sadhguru, this morning you said that yoga actually 'hastens one's evolution.' Can you elaborate? I know this is happening to me, but how is it possible and what exactly is happening?"

"There is a beautiful story about a caterpillar that illustrates this," Sadhguru said. "Have you heard that story before?"

"No, I am not familiar with it."

"This caterpillar lived much of its life believing it had come into being only to eat and sleep and do what the rest of the caterpillars did. However, this particular caterpillar was restless and unhappy, and he felt incomplete. Somehow he sensed that life had a dimension not yet experienced.

"One day, driven by a strange longing he could neither define nor fulfill, the restless fellow became still and silent. He hung from the branch of a tree and wove and wove, weaving a cocoon around himself. Inside the cocoon, although constrained and uncomfortable, he waited, sensing and aware. His patience eventually bore fruit, for when the cocoon burst open, lo and behold, he was no longer the lowly worm that wove darkness around himself but a resplendent, winged butterfly whose very colors dazzled the appreciative sky. Now he soared and flew, no longer limited to a worm-like existence, but free and unchained. The caterpillar had been transformed into a thing of lightness and air, magic and beauty.

"Once the transformation had taken place, it was impossible for the butterfly to return to being a worm. In the cocoon, the caterpillar had become one with his inner being, and in this union of the body and the divine he reached his ultimate nature." Sadhguru paused, his eyes alive and sparkling, and then he said, "What happened in the cocoon can be described as yoga."

He paused for a moment before saying, "Here I must say that it really amused me recently to hear a top-level neuroscientist tell me that within twenty-four hours we can completely rewire our brains—that within a day we can change the very fundamentals of our life. He went on to add that the neuron activity in the brain is of the highest possibility when our spine is erect and our body is still. This is something we have known for ages!"

Then Sadhguru asked me if I had heard that some researchers in India had been scanning the brains of people who have been through Isha Yoga's Inner Engineering course and practicing the techniques for more than three months.

I had heard about that, so I nodded yes.

Sadhguru went on to say that the scientists had found that the coherence between the practitioners' right and left brain was phenomenally high. "That means, Cheryl, that you will get to use a little more of your brain than before. Generally they say that people are only using 12 percent of their brain, but from my experience of people, I don't believe they are using even that," he said and let out a hoot of infectious laughter.

Then he went on, "Yoga is the path of becoming limitless. Yoga transforms and liberates human beings so that they can reach this unbounded state. Humans, unlike animals, do not merely exist. They are becoming. 'Human' is not an established quality; one has to grow into it. One has to become that. To evolve as a human being is to become aware of one's limitations, to strive, with intense passion, toward the transcendence for which we all have the potential. Yoga is a way of finding your ultimate potential. In a specific context, yoga has come to mean spiritual union with the absolute. Liberation while living is the goal of yoga, the highest experience, a fusion of the individual with the universal."

Although his words seemed both inspiring and filled with possibility, I caught myself again wondering if such transcendence really could be possible for me. Even though many remarkable things had happened to me, I continued to wonder if I would truly be able to become self-realized in this lifetime. Part of me wondered how much the yoga, the practices, had to do with it. It's a technology that affects not only your body, mind, and energy, but that also somehow makes you receptive. I know it is a big part of it, but I also know it is not the whole thing. Some of the practices Sadhguru teaches are similar to those I was exposed to in the past, but he puts them together in a completely different way. Even with all the yoga Sadhguru did in previous lifetimes, and with all that he accomplished, he said he did not become enlightened. The reason why is shrouded in mystery. I knew the practices were working, but perhaps this process is more than something I can do myself. Something seems to have to happen that *I'm* not doing. I have often heard Sadhguru say that "you have to put yourself aside."

Perhaps the answer to this question could be found in Sadhguru's own story. Still curious as to how he had come to yoga in this lifetime, I asked him, "Did you have a yoga teacher this time around?"

"Yes, when I was just eleven years of age, the grace of my guru found expression in the form of an ageless yogi. He was a seventy-eight-year-old boy at the time and he lived on to a very active 108 years of age. This yogi was a direct disciple of my revered guru. He came as an unknown reminder to me of my guru's will to create an eternal energy form. He taught me some very simple yoga practices. After that, this simple form of yoga just began to happen every day for the next thirteen years. The reason I am saying that it just happened is because I was not committed to the discipline, but without one single day's break, it just happened from within me to create a very strong and stable body and mind under any situation. No matter where I was, every day without fail I did the yoga. Since then there has been no looking back. Life has moved at a fast-forward pace from one peak to another, assisted and enhanced by the grace of a glorious being."

"Who was this yoga teacher" I asked.

"This yogi who taught me a few simple practices was named Malladi Halli Swami."

"What was he like?"

"He was an incredible human being. He was a yogi, a bodybuilder, and also an expert in various martial arts. In addition to those accomplishments, he was a great *ayurvedic* doctor, or healer using an ancient art. He was a *nadivaidya,* which is someone who can diagnose disease simply by feeling the pulse. He could not only tell what was going on in your system today, he could tell what diseases you would get in the next fifteen years. He would tell you right now, and what's more, he would tell you what corrective measures to take.

"He used to come to the town where my grandparents lived and camp at their house. It was a very large house—the house itself was almost an acre in size—and in the backyard there was a large well."

"What do you mean by 'large well'?" I could not remember having seen any large wells in this country.

"All those old homes had wells in the backyards. This well was about eight feet in diameter and dropped to about 150 feet. In the summer, the water was about sixty to seventy feet down. One of the sports we did as children for fun was to jump into the well and climb out.

Climbing out was a big part of the challenge. There were no stairs; you had to hold on to the rocks and spider your way up.

"If you did not jump carefully, your brains could become a smear on the wall. So we jumped in and climbed out, jumped in and climbed out. Only a few of the boys could do it. One day this seventy-something-year-old man came. He looked at us and then jumped into the well, and he climbed out faster than me. I did not like that. This man was not just old, he was ancient to me. So I asked him, 'Okay, how?'

"He said to me, 'You come and do yoga.' That's how I got into yoga this time.

"Swami was such an incredible human being. The way he lived was remarkable. Six days a week he traveled and only one day a week he stayed in his ashram. He maintained that schedule for ninety years of his life. Monday mornings he was always at the ashram because that was the day he sat as an *ayurvedic* doctor. He began his day at three thirty or four o'clock in the morning and went on until eight at night. Once he sat down to treat his patients that was it. He didn't get up for food, toilet, this, that. Nothing.

"The volunteers who came to help him arrived in shifts, but he would just sit there for eighteen hours straight. And for every patient who came, he had a joke to tell. This was not like a doctor-patient thing at all; this was more like a festival. Most people forgot that they even had a disease in his presence.

"The next six days he would be traveling, most of the time lecturing, demonstrating, and fundraising. He was definitely one yogi who was not afraid of money. He spent a lot of time fundraising because at that time he had three thousand destitute children with him, whom he was feeding and educating. You know what is involved in feeding and educating just one child.

"When I had been doing yoga with him for six or seven years, the other boys and I used to get into the wrestling ring with him. I had been working out in a gymnasium and I jogged more than twelve kilometers a day, so at the time I was all muscle and very fit. There were a few boys who were stronger than me, but I was also considered very quick. I could even catch a snake; not just any snake, but a provoked cobra when it was trying to attack. I would catch it with my hands without a stick or anything. Even now I can do it. I was so quick, but if I got into the ring with Swami, it was no good. He always got the better of me.

"To even the score we began to pit three boys against him. He was in his eighties and we three young, strong, quick boys never lasted a minute. Within seconds he would have all three of us pinned down. Not once did we last a minute with him. So, we used to joke with him about when he was going to die. We'd ask him, 'The way you're going, when will you go? It looks like we will pass you and go. When are you going?'

"He would very confidently say, 'I have another forty years of work before I finish and go.' He was almost super human. The way he was going it looked like he was going to fulfill that, but at the age of 108, he passed away.

"To give you an example of the incredible way he lived and his commitment to what he was doing, one night when he was around eighty he got to the railway station a little late in the evening. It was a Sunday evening. No matter where he was on Sunday, he was always back in the ashram Monday morning to see patients.

"So, this Sunday evening he was in a town called Arasikere, which is about seventy kilometers (or forty-three miles) away, and the railway was on strike. There was no train and no other way to get to the ashram. There were two companions with him. When he saw that the trains were not operating, he just left his companions standing on the railway platform and took off running down the tracks. Overnight he ran the entire seventy kilometers and reached the ashram early Monday morning to treat his patients. People in the ashram did not realize how he got there until later, when the other two people arrived and said, 'Swamiji ran away on the railway tracks!'

"At the age of 108, on a certain day, Swami was in Mysore city giving a lecture when he collapsed on the dais. He had some kind of a cardiac attack. We don't know how major or minor it was. When they admitted him to the hospital, he was unconscious.

"They put him in the ICU, which was on the second floor. Somewhere in the middle of the night, he became conscious and saw all the tubes and needles they put in his body. This was not acceptable to him. He had never been in a hospital before. He just pulled out everything and escaped through the window and ran away. A 108-year-old man jumped out of a second-floor window and got away! Three months later he died. Such an incredible human being he was.

"Yet, when this incredible man was a child of eight or nine, you would never have been able to recognize what he would become. He was such a chronic asthmatic that his parents were convinced he was going to die, and die very young. He was not growing right and was very small for his age. When a great yogi happened to come to their area, they went and handed their child over to him and said, 'Please, try to do something for him.' Swami took the boy in out of compassion, and he lived with this yogi for several years. The yogi brought up the boy. In the care of this divine yogi, the boy grew incredibly."

As Sadhguru told this story, a new question occurred to me. Having heard so many stories about the benefits of yoga, now I wondered why Sadhguru seemed to discount the yoga he practiced in his past lifetime, when he was called Shiva Yogi.

"Sadhguru," I said, "last night you told us that the yoga that Shiva Yogi did was of no relevance to you. Why is that? I mean, it worked, didn't it?"

After considering my question, he said, "It worked to a point. But it was still no good, when all you want is ultimate realization. Nothing else matters. Do you want God or just to receive his gifts? Shiva Yogi was able to raise his energy up to his third eye, or Agna chakra, but he was not able to attain the final realization, so he remained a forlorn seeker."

I had heard some stories about Sadhguru's most recent past lifetime—the next birth after he was known as Shiva Yogi. There are many stories floating around about that lifetime because it was so recent and is particularly relevant to his life this time around. Some people even have memories of being with him then. In that lifetime, he was also a guru called Sadhguru. His full name was Sadhguru Shree Brahma. He was known as a *chakreswara,* one who has absolute mastery over all the chakras (the energy system). But, I didn't know what any of that meant.

"How do the chakras tie into all this?" I had read in many places that there are seven main chakras in the human body, and that they are energy centers, but I did not know anything else about them or what relevance they might have, let alone how they work or affect us.

When I asked this question, something about Sadhguru changed: His presence became marked by a charged intensity that was audible in his voice, as it often is when he addresses certain topics. I had visited Sadhguru Shree Brahma's ashram in Coimbatore, not too far from the Isha Yoga ashram. Although it is very small and not very well kept, the presence—the energy—in the place completely floored me. I never used to be very sensitive to anything like this. The very thought of the place even now sends an electric feeling up my spine.

I was snapped out of my reverie when Sadhguru began to speak in response to my question.

"What we call 'chakras' are energy centers in the body," he began. "Seven is the number of chakras most people have heard about, but there are actually 114 chakras in the body.

"Even though you have yet to realize it, the human body is a complex energy form. In addition to the chakras, it has seventy-two thousand energy channels called *nadis*. These channels are the pathways along which the vital energy moves. They meet at different points in the body and form a triangle. We call this triangle a chakra, which means 'wheel.' We call it a chakra, or wheel, because it symbolizes growth, dynamism, and movement. So, even though it is actually a triangle, we call it a chakra. Some of these centers are very powerful while others are not as powerful. At different levels, these energy centers produce different qualities in a human being.

"Fundamentally, any spiritual path can be described as a journey from the base chakra, called the Mooladhara chakra and located at the base of the spine, to the Sahasrar chakra, located at the top of the head. The seven chakras are called Mooladhara, Swadhisthana, Manipuraka, Anahata, Vishuddhi, Agna, and Sahasrar.

"This journey of movement from the Mooladhara chakra to the Sahasrar chakra is from one dimension to another. This may happen in many different ways. All the different yoga practices can effect this movement. Fundamentally, you can describe any spiritual path as a journey from the lowest to the highest chakra. Mooladhara means the fundamental, or foundation. It is the very fulcrum of life, the very basis of life. It is located at the base of your spine. You cannot live without being active in this base chakra, but you can live without being active in the Sahasrar chakra.

"Mooladhara is really made up of two terms: *Moola* means the root or source and *adhar* means the foundation. So, it is the very basic foundation of life. In this physical body, your energies need to be to some extent in the Mooladhara chakra. Otherwise, you cannot exist.

But, if the Mooladhara chakra alone is dominant, food and sleep will be the predominant factors in your life.

"We can speak in terms of lower and higher chakras, but such language is often and too easily misunderstood. It is like saying the foundation of a building and the roof of a building. The roof of the building is not superior to the foundation of the building. The foundation of the building is more basic to the building than the roof. The quality, the life span, and the stability and security of the building depend to a large extent on its foundation rather than on its roof. But in terms of language, the roof is higher, and the foundation is lower.

"The next chakra is called Swadhisthana. If your energies move into Swadhisthana, you are a pleasure seeker. The Swadhisthana chakra is located just above the genital organs. When this chakra is active, you enjoy the physical world in so many ways. If you look at a pleasure seeker, you see that his life and his experience of life are just a little more intense compared to a person who is only about food and sleep.

"If your energy moves into the Manipuraka chakra, you are a doer in the world. You are all about action. You can do many, many things. You are endless activity. If your energies move into the Anahata chakra, you are a creative person, a person who is creative in nature, or an artist, or an actor, or someone who lives very intensely—

more intensely, perhaps, than a businessman, who is all action.

"The Anahata literally means the 'un-struck.' If you want to make any sound, you have to strike two objects together. The un-struck sound is called Anahata. Anahata is like a transition between your survival instincts and the instinct to liberate your self. It is located in the heart area. The lower three chakras are mainly concerned with your physical existence. Anahata is a combination: It is a meeting place for both the survival and the enlightenment chakras.

"Then Vishuddhi—a word that literally means a filter. Vishuddhi is located in the area of your throat. If your energies move into Vishuddhi, you become a very powerful human being, but this power is not just political or administrative. A person can be powerful in many ways. A person can become so powerful that if he just sits in one place, things will happen for him. He can manifest life beyond the limitations of time and space.

"If your energies move into the Agna chakra, located between your eyebrows, you are intellectually enlightened. You have attained to a new balance and peace within you. The outside no longer disturbs you, but you are still experientially not liberated.

"If your energies move into Sahasrar, you become ecstatic beyond all reason. You will simply burst with ecstasy for no reason whatsoever.

"All these chakras have more than one dimension to them. One dimension is a physical existence—a biological existence—and they also have a spiritual dimension. So, all these chakras can be transformed into a completely different dimension. If you bring the right kind of awareness, the same Mooladhara that is food and sleep will turn into the process of becoming absolutely free from the process of food and sleep. If one wants to go beyond food and sleep, one needs Mooladhara in an evolved state.

"To move from Mooladhara to Agna requires many procedures, many methods, processes through which one can raise one's energies. From Agna to Sahasrar, there is no path. You can only jump there. In a way you have to fall upward. So, the question of going step by step to that dimension does not really arise. There is no way. It is because of this one aspect that the spiritual traditions have emphasized the significance of the guru's role in one's realization. You can only jump into an abyss the depth of which you do not know if you have an absolutely insane heart, or if your trust in someone is so deep you are willing to do anything in his presence. Most people, due to a lack of either of these two aspects, just get stuck in Agna chakra. Then, peacefulness is the highest thing that they will know. It is only from this limitation that there has been so much talk about peace being the highest possibility."

"Sadhguru," I asked, "what does this have to do with *kundalini?*"

"The most fundamental energy within you is called *kundalini.* To fulfill our survival needs, just a miniscule amount of this energy is needed. Most of the energy within you is untapped or unaroused. We refer to this energy as *kundalini,* symbolized as a coiled snake.

"The reason a snake is used for symbolism is because when a snake is still, it is absolutely still. Only when it moves do you notice it. That is the nature of a snake. So, *kundalini* is referred to as a coiled snake because this energy, which is so tremendous, exists within you, but until it moves, you will never realize it is there. Once the energy is aroused, it does many things to you."

I certainly know how the practices, the methods, I learned from him that were supposed to cause this energy to move had affected my health. There was no denying the results of my blood tests before and after. The doctor thought it was astonishing. It also provides an explanation for some of the things that I've experienced, like when things seem much more vivid than usual, as if my perception is much deeper and everything is pulsating with a vibrant energy. I've experienced this at sacred spots in the Himalayas and also in my day-to-day life. Everything has gotten crisper and more vibrant.

"In yogic culture, very systematic methods for tapping this energy exist. When your energy moves, you cannot believe that this is you. Something enormous begins to happen. It becomes a tremendous force within. So, if this *kundalini* moves to different dimensions of your body, or your chakras, it affects different aspects of your life in so many ways. . . ."

Sadhguru fell silent, as if he had said enough for now. Sensing that it was time to change the subject, after a few moments I asked, "So, what happened to Shiva Yogi?"

Sadhguru continued with the story. "Even though Shiva Yogi was exposed to a variety of *sadhana* and methods, and had mastered the same, he became stagnant after reaching the level of the Agna chakra. The final realization, after so much effort, had still not happened. Then he saw a divine guru and at that moment, he recognized that this guru was at the absolute peak of consciousness.

"Until then he had not found a guru that could lead him to the ultimate. Even though he had met many people who were at heightened levels of consciousness, he would not accept another man as a guru. He only wanted Shiva to come and initiate him. Shiva was known as the highest. For him, Shiva was the only guru.

"To Shiva Yogi, Shiva was God himself. Only if Shiva appeared would he accept a guru; otherwise, he stuck to his *sadhana*. But, when he saw this divine guru and recognized that he was at the very peak of consciousness, he became completely receptive to him.

"Even though he was able to open himself to the guru to an extent, there was still some resistance in him because he could only completely open to Shiva. The guru, an enlightened yogi who saw the intensity in Shiva Yogi and his struggle to surpass Agna chakra, out of his compassion used his walking stick and lightly tapped Shiva Yogi's forehead between the eyebrows.

"In that moment, Shiva Yogi merged into his ultimate nature. But, a childlike longing in him still craved to see Shiva. The divine guru, out of his compassion, catered to this childlike need and took the form of Shiva himself. Shiva Yogi's contact with his guru was very brief in the physical sense, and after that they never met again. But, they remained in touch in a different way.

"Somehow, the divine guru identified Shiva Yogi as a person suitable and capable of carrying out a gift he wanted to offer to humanity: the establishing of an energy form, a *linga,* of immense proportions that would aid people in bringing about unobstructed spiritual transformation. This is an energy form that would always be available to people who wanted to evolve their consciousness. This was a gift the divine guru wanted to make available to humanity. Before leaving his body, he conveyed a vision of the eternal form to Shiva Yogi and entrusted this work to him. This was not done in speech, not in words. He communicated that this needed to be done, and he transmitted the technology to him.

"Shiva Yogi immediately began working toward fulfilling this mission ordained by his guru. For many reasons, he was unable to complete his guru's vision in that lifetime. Out of unfailing gratitude, his desire to establish this sacred energy form and fulfill his guru's wishes set Shiva Yogi on a course that took two more lifetimes."

After enlightenment, Sadhguru said, one generally ends the cycle of birth and death on the physical plane. But, because of the work of creating an eternal form, which came to be known as the Dhyanalinga, Shiva Yogi made the rare choice to reincarnate and continue his physical sojourn.

When I asked Sadhguru why there were not more enlightened beings on the planet, he said that for most beings, the moment of enlightenment happens at the time of leaving the body. I read that even Buddha, after his enlightenment, chose not to come back for another earthly sojourn when it was time for him to go. After Buddha awakened, he wrote the following poem:

Seeking but not finding the House Builder,
I traveled through the round of countless births:
O painful is birth ever and again.

House Builder, you have now been seen;
You shall not build the house again.
Your rafters have been broken down;
Your ridgepole is demolished too.

My mind has now attained the unformed nirvana
And reached the end of every kind of craving.

Then Buddha's next thought was, "I have attained the unborn. My liberation is unassailable. This is my last birth. There will now be no renewal of becoming."

As I was wondering what it could possibly mean not to be identified with our bodies and personalities, and just what liberation actually means, I started thinking about Shiva Yogi's divine guru. I wondered why something did not seem to add up. Then I realized that Sadhguru had mentioned him earlier in relationship to his yoga teacher in this lifetime. I could not see how Sadhguru's guru from another lifetime could also be Malladi Halli Swami's guru in this lifetime. I asked, "Are you saying that the guru who liberated you two lifetimes ago was your yoga teacher's guru in this lifetime?"

Sadhguru said, "Yes, he had the same guru as me."

"How is that possible?" I asked.

"My divine guru actually lived 150, 160 years," Sadhguru answered.

I had heard many extraordinary tales about yogis before, living even hundreds of years, but I never thought that it was actually possible. I remembered reading in Yogananda's *The Autobiography of a Yogi* about many such possibilities that yogis had explored and manifested. Even though I am generally open-minded, I am always skeptical about such things and had thought these stories were just symbolic and not factual—until now.

"This convergence of gurus could not have been a coincidence," I said.

Sadhguru laughed. "Yes," he said. "It was more like an insurance policy."

"Are you saying that because your guru wanted to see the Dhyanalinga happen, he was somehow involved again in your life this time? How is that possible?"

"Cheryl, when your consciousness is no longer identified with your body and mind, many things are possible. Many things that seem like 'miracles' become possible."

"Sadhguru," I asked, "but how are miracles possible?"

"So, you are asking now what a miracle is?" Sadhguru responded. "Miracles are always within the laws of nature, but those laws are not now on your current level of perception. They involve something that is happening, genuinely happening, though you are not able to understand or grasp how. You see the result, but you are unable to see the process.

"Is it so difficult to understand that someone may have a different level of perception and capabilities? Even animals have a different level of perception than you. During the tsunami, all the animals went to higher ground. They have a different perception than people.

"If you did not know anything about electricity or how it produces light, and you looked at this torch light, as far as you were concerned, it would be just a piece of metal. If I told you that this thing would produce light, would you believe me? You would not, but if I flooded this place with light, it would be a 'miracle.' You would probably think that I was God or his son, or at least a messenger. So, various things that people around me talk about, things that have happened to them, it is just that they are unable to figure out how they happened. Existence is in many different dimensions, not just the physical. For those who live and know only the physical, everything that is beyond the physical seems miraculous.

"These so-called miracles can happen in many ways. When you were born, your body was so little, and now it has become big. Pardon me!" he said, smiling, "I am not saying that you are big! So, this growth happened from within you. This body was created from within. You gave it the material in the form of food. The creation process happened from within.

"That which is the basis of creation, the creator, is within you. When the manufacturer of this body is within you, if you have some repair job that needs to be done, should you go to the manufacturer or to the local mechanic?

"I have just introduced you to the manufacturer, so do not blame me for the miracles. I always play down the miracles because I don't want people to come here for miracles. I want them here with genuine seeking.

"The Dhyanalinga is created as an external manifestation of the peak form of all inner energy. How it aids and contributes in the evolution of consciousness is difficult to explain. It may take several hundred years before its true value is recognized. There have been many attempts by other yogis to create a Dhyanalinga. It is something that was known in India, but it was lost over the centuries."

Sadhguru became quiet in his other-worldly way, so it was some time before I felt comfortable asking him to say more about this. The fire was dying down, so I placed a few more logs on the flames. Leela seemed to have drifted into meditation, as she often does when Sadhguru goes into a certain frame of being, as if not wanting to miss a single opportunity to ride the wave of his energies.

After a while I ventured, "Sadhguru, what exactly is a *linga*? Before I met you, I had never heard the word."

"In Sanskrit," Sadhguru replied, patiently as always, "*linga* literally means the form. Any form or symbol can be referred to as a *linga*. It is a symbol of the unbounded.

The expression of religious and philosophical ideas through symbols has come naturally to people since ancient times in many parts of the world. The *linga* is an ellipsoid, or the first form. It is also true that if one raises one's energies to their highest pitch before dissolution, the final form that it takes on is also an ellipsoid, or the *linga.* Even Galileo spoke about the ellipsoid aspect of the universe. When universes are formed, the ellipsoid shape is the first form taken. A *linga* can be a naturally occurring form, such as a rock, or it can be a form that is created. The shape of the *linga* allows it to function as a perennial storehouse of energy. Most *lingas* are energized through the chanting of mantras."

Sadhguru's appearance completely changed when he spoke about this energy form. Somehow he seemed to expand. His physical presence became mountain-like in stature; he seemed to spread out with a spiritual radiance that was ageless, ancient, and timeless. Looking at him, I had a feeling similar to that I've had gazing up at high mountain peaks, so enormous and powerful you feel overwhelmed and you have to step back. It takes your breath away. He seems unapproachable at these times, and my strong instinct is to keep a certain distance. He is often like this during his advanced programs. My friends and I have often talked about how it's as if he steps out of personality much the way a person removes a coat. He becomes something enormous, unlike any other human I have ever met. In other situations, he's much more approachable. I think it is out of his kindness, not wanting us to be uncomfortable around him, that he keeps himself cloaked. This was one of those times when he was unmasked.

The Dhyanalinga was created at the ashram in India by Sadhguru, and there are many wild stories told by the people that were there when it was being created. (They were seeing and hearing all kinds of unbelievable things.) It is an energy form that is encased in an ellipsoid structure. The structure is enclosed by a beautiful dome building, which creates the Dhyanalinga temple. It is a wonderful space to sit and meditate. But, no matter what I had read about it or who I asked, it was still something that I could not understand. I wanted to hear about it from Sadhguru.

"What is the Dhyanalinga and how does it function? Is there a logical explanation?" I asked.

"The Dhyanalinga is a tremendous tool for transformation. Generally, people are unable to recognize the full potential and value of what it is. It is the highest possible manifestation of the divine. It has all seven chakras functioning fully. Sitting at the Dhyanalinga is the same as sitting with a live guru—without all the confusion. The consecration of a Dhyanalinga has always posed problems because the deliberate energizing of a form is a complex and difficult process."

Before my experience with the Dhyanalinga in India, I always thought that talk of energy forms was just new age hocus pocus or some imagined idea. In fact, if I heard about this from anyone other than Sadhguru, I would never have believed anything about it. I did not think energy forms existed. Once, when I told Sadhguru that I didn't believe in energy forms, he looked at me with widened eyes and asked, "Why not? You are one."

Now, based on my own experiences, I know that the Dhyanalinga possesses a powerful energy. When I first sat in the Dhyanalinga, I absolutely loved being in that space. It is so beautiful there, and somehow deep. But, I did not think much about it other than that it was a wonderful place to meditate. Only after I was in there a few more times did something seem to happen. It actually felt alive and palpable in there. I have never been particularly meditative, so I was stunned when I looked at my watch and saw that hours had passed. Only then did I really begin to wonder just what it was all about. I was sure that I had only been there a few minutes. Suddenly, it was dark outside. All that time had just disappeared. I still don't understand how it works, but the more I am around Sadhguru and the more such experiences I have, the more I am convinced that he helps us to access a dimension that most of us don't even know exists, much less have access to.

The fire had begun to weaken, and so Leela got up and threw some more wood on it. Sparks flew up and popped above the flames. When Leela sat back down, I turned to Sadhguru, who was peacefully gazing at the sky.

"Sadhguru, will you tell us more of the story? You left off with Shiva Yogi's enlightenment and his mission of the Dhyanalinga. What happened next?"

"Having received the grace of the great guru to be an instrument in fulfilling the guru's monumental mission, having received this fiat, Shiva Yogi immediately started endeavoring to accomplish the same. But, as he plunged into the preliminary steps of preparing his own system toward this goal, he realized that the appropriate time for this Dhyanalinga to happen was yet to be. He spent a few years doing the necessary preliminary work and then shed his body so he could come at an appropriate time with a more youthful physicality. And thus, Sadhguru Shree Bhramha was born in Tamil Nadu in South India.

"Sadhguru Shree Bhramha, having recognized that the guru, the light of his life, had consciously shed his body on the White Mountains of Vellingiri, started striving to establish and consecrate the eternal form at the foothills of those mountains.

"Sadhguru Shree Bhramha, born with the sole purpose of establishing this eternal form, made himself a fiery person of immense intensity. As he saw that an endeavor of this magnitude could not be accomplished without social support, he went about establishing seventy institutions in that state, including schools, orphanages, and ashrams.

"At the same time, he started working on a select group of disciples who would be needed in consecrating the eternal form of the Dhyanalinga. This esoteric endeavor brought a certain amount of resistance from a few powerful families in the area, and it became increasingly difficult for Sadhguru to continue his work. As the resisting group of people started persecuting his disciples, Sadhguru again realized that he was not yet going to be able to fulfill his guru's will. Sadhguru had not planned to stay in his body a moment longer than was needed to establish the Dhyanalinga; he had planned to live for only forty-two years. For the purpose of the Dhyanalinga, he had set his life energies in a fiery intensity that would burn itself out in that amount of time. So, with the time set for his departure, running into social difficulties put his monumental endeavor into jeopardy.

"As the time ticked away, even though Sadhguru was an accomplished yogi of enormous capabilities, a certain directionless anger arose in him. It became apparent that he would again be leaving without fulfilling the sacred mission that was placed upon him. With his spirit on fire he walked like a cannonball without rest or respite, followed by one lone disciple, more than six hundred kilometers toward the Somashwar Temple at Kadapa in the state of Andra Pradesh. This is the temple where the guru had spent a certain period of time, so Sadhguru was seeking to go into the lap of his Master.

"He spent several months there putting together an elaborate plan of how he and a few of his people would come back for another lifetime. This planning went to the extent of deciding who should be born where and in which womb, and he planted his people in families that had been the source of resistance.

"When this elaborate, esoteric procedure was complete and in place, he walked back to Coimbatore. After he spent a little time with his disciples, for the last time he went up the sacred mountain of Vellingiri. This was a grand temple to him, as his guru had not only walked upon that magnificent mountain but he also chose to shed his mortal coil there. At the time of parting from his disciples, with a determined assurance he declared, 'I will be back.' He went up the mountain and spent a day and a half preparing his system to create a rare phenomenon of leaving his body through all seven chakras, which was a way of demonstrating that he was fully qualified to create the eternal form and that the unwanted postponement was only due to his inability to handle the unknowing social elements around him.

"When Sadhguru returned again to create the eternal form, once he remembered it, he was determined to construct himself in a socially savvy way, even though he still carried the same fiery spirit and intensity."

Now Sadhguru spoke no more, and—just as I had discovered after visiting the Dhyanalinga for the first time—I became aware that many hours had passed since we came to our island, although they had seemed only minutes. It was as if the time had disappeared. In deep silence, we loaded the boat and headed for shelter as I pondered all that had been said.

CHAPTER EIGHT
Our Last Night: A Deeper Understanding

"Self-realization is not given to you by the guru. He simply removes the obstacles that are beyond your perception."
—Sadhguru

The next morning was made to order, an exquisite day with colors so vivid and air so fresh, it felt as if we were in paradise. Even though our last few evenings had begun earlier and earlier and I understood that Sadhguru's focus during the day was elsewhere, I still wanted him to experience this place outside with us on this gorgeous day. Fortunately, it was as if fate knew how much I wanted to prolong what little time we had left with him and helped to make that happen. Leela and I did get to have some of the guru's treasured company in the daytime for a relished change, although this seemed more impromptu than planned.

Early that morning, Sadhguru got a call from India, and the caller said it was important that they speak to him. To relay the message, I went to his room and knocked lightly on his door. I did not want to disturb him, but the door was cracked a little, so when he did not answer, I peaked in. Not surprisingly, he was sitting cross-legged on the rough-hewn, Native Indian rug I'd placed on the hardwood floor. He looked fully absorbed and out of reach. I felt as if he was not here at all. I quickly and quietly closed the door and left.

Sadhguru came downstairs about an hour later and got involved on the phone and then the Internet. He had almost two hundred e-mails. Talk about a busy mystic! Since we had seen so little of him in the daylight hours, I asked whether he would like for me to arrange a golf game for him with my neighbor, who I knew was a scratch golfer. He said yes. I was happy he would get to enjoy some outside fun. I hated to see him missing all these balmy days we were having, and I knew that golf was one of the more Western customs he was beginning to enjoy.

In fact, during his last trip to the United States a few months earlier I saw him play his third game of golf. He seemed to love it. He was great at it. If anything was an advertisement for yoga, watching Sadhguru master golf was. I heard a commentary once of some golf instructor trying to explain how he teaches people to get in "the zone" while playing golf. I have never seen Sadhguru any other way but in the zone. I love watching him play games since it is such a contrast to how we see him during a program. He is so ancient, mystical, and often otherworldly when you sit in front of him that the childlike exuberance, intensity, and athletic accuracy he has when he plays a game is quite a surprise. If Sadhguru takes anything seriously, it is games. He really plays to win.

The guys he was playing with for that game were some businessmen who were also Isha meditators and who knew that Sadhguru had only golfed twice before. They were pretty good golfers (or so they thought), and they considered it their duty to teach Sadhguru this American game, to "help the guru learn to golf." The outcome of that day of golf was, however, not what they expected.

Despite his radiant skin and flowing beard, the splash Sadhguru made on the golf course was not because of his appearance, but his way of playing golf. Sadhguru seemed to like only one particular club, a wood with a large striking face. In addition to trying to tell him how to hold the club and how to bend his knees, these "proud golfers" were explaining to Sadhguru why he should use a variety of different clubs. Sadhguru said, "Leave that to me. Just tell me where the ball should go." These guys just weren't getting the hint and persistently kept giving him instructions. They stopped only when he finally said, "Can't I just hit the ball? I know how to whack a ball; just tell me where it should go."

At this point his partners relented and gave him the club he wanted, and he promptly hit the ball 265 yards on the green. Everyone's mouths fell open, and Leela and I tried not to laugh too loudly. From that point on, the instruction stopped and the competition began. That day, with the exception of a couple of mulligans, Sadhguru ended with a score of three under par. No one on the green or later in the clubhouse had ever heard of such an outcome for a novice, especially one with such an unconventional way of playing the game.

Disappointingly, the golf game did not happen this day at the lake because no one was at home at my neighbor's house. Sadhguru was fine with that and instead said he was eager to take the wave runners out for a ride. I thought he might have been. I knew his agenda this week must have been very important to him, or he would already have been on those boats. The boats were new, and when we picked them out, my son got involved and made sure I got the ones that would go very fast. To me, they sped along like rockets.

Now that Sadhguru had chosen this activity, the three of us quickly changed our clothes and tromped down to the dock equipped with life vests, keys, and towels.

Sadhguru hopped on the water scooter, and as I was telling him what to do, he took off. By the time Leela and I could untie the other boat, Sadhguru was completely out of sight, going at least sixty miles an hour. We took off after him although we might as well have been tracking a ghost!

We had great fun on the boats that day, with Leela screaming as we went as fast as we could stand. The day was exquisite. The sun was warm and the sky brilliant. Splashing along the water, I couldn't imagine a more splendid afternoon. While we were out on the lake, Sadhguru pointed out a different island for our evening fireside chat. As much as I enjoyed the spectacular day, I still could hardly wait for the night. I loved our nights.

After a few hours, we returned home. Sadhguru once again went behind closed doors, and Leela and I went back to the dock to hang out and talk. Earlier in the day, Sadhguru had mentioned a different visit he had once taken to the Appalachian Mountains and how beautiful it was in this other location also. I asked Leela if she knew where Sadhguru had been and she said he had visited a place called Center Hill Lake, which is a few hours drive from Nashville. She said it was quite pristine and secluded there, an area where you can go for days without seeing another human face. Leela went on to say that it was there that Sadhguru wrote the poem called "America." I remembered that stirring poem and I was curious about it. It is a haunting piece that touches on the terrible fate of the Native American people, who were defeated and shamed. When I asked Leela if she knew what the circumstances were that inspired the poem, she said that before writing it, Sadhguru had taken a walk alone in the forest and when he returned, he seemed distant and unapproachable.

"I have known him for so many years, but this day he was different," she said. "When he walked into the cottage after his absence of a couple of hours, he seemed very intense. He was so out of time and out of place it was like he was not there at all, but he was also so much there. I know I am not making sense, but his image that day has stayed with me." Later, she said, he explained what happened during his walk in the forest, but Leela did not want to tell the story to me, preferring that I get it from Sadhguru.

The incident Leela related made me wonder again what life is like for Sadhguru, what he can see and know that is out of our experience. I decided that I would ask him about the poem that night. I also wanted to ask him about a curious encounter I had with Ram Dass, when I, too, had seen things way out of the ordinary. In part, my experience with Ram Dass was what also made Sadhguru seem so familiar to me when I first set eyes on him and felt that pull in my spine. Now, after our talk about chakras and *kundalini*, I wanted to sort out what had happened during that exceptional time I had with Ram Dass. In part, I was seeing some explanations for the different ways in which we can experience life and other dimensions.

As soon as we settled in by the fire that night, I asked Sadhguru if it would be okay for me to get his insight into something that had happened to me. Even as I said that, I was uncomfortable bringing up a personal question, but I persisted because this was an experience I had carried around inside for a long time. As I knew he would, Sadhguru made it clear that it was okay to ask.

So, I sat there mentally phrasing my question, aware of the warm fire and the frog symphony and the owls calling around us. The thing was I was not sure I could even describe what happened. When I was still quite young, twenty-two to be exact, I had many burning questions. By this time, I had read much about yoga, enlightenment, and Eastern religions, and I had had both psychedelic experiences and some unusual experiences during meditation. Because of what I had read and experienced, I was convinced that somehow there was much more to us than the physical and that God is not some kindly grandfather off in some remote place.

I knew that science says that all matter is contained energy, that everything physical can be reduced to energy and that energy cannot be destroyed. The more esoteric my studies became, the more I seemed to be reading in more than one place that there is only one God and that God has taken the form of the many and that underneath all us is God, and we just did not know it. My mind was constantly grappling with that.

So, the burning question I had when I met with Ram Dass was, How can we possibly all be one when I feel and experience life so separately? Yet, somehow I knew that everything was connected. I had heard life described as Maya, or illusion. That always made me angry. It seemed so cold and callous. Life seemed too brutal to be passed off as some mere movie, so to speak. I thought it was way too painful to be called unreal, but I also was constantly aware of the transitory nature of things. So, what is real? I wondered. What doesn't die? God? Was there something real that I was and could somehow know?

Well, all this turmoil was with me when I sat down with Ram Dass. At that time, he had not been back from India for very long. He was quite magnificent. He had spent a lot of time with his guru, Neem Karoli Baba, and had done a lot of spiritual work. Some of my friends had moved to New York City to be with him, and they called to tell me that he was going to be in Atlanta and that I should go talk to him. I was a little reserved in those days, but something propelled me to approach him after the talk he gave in Stone Mountain, which is part of metropolitan Atlanta. When I asked Ram Dass if he would have any time to meet with me, he looked up at the ceiling a few minutes and said, "Yes, okay. Come to the Stone Mountain Inn tomorrow." He gave me the time, place, and room number. The next day I was there with bells on.

I knocked on the door, and Ram Dass told me to come in. When I opened the door, he was sitting cross-legged on the motel bed. I asked him if he was taking a break, and he said, "It is all a break." I thought that must be very nice for him since, for me, life seemed to be somewhat of a struggle. Anyway, he told me to come in and pull up a chair. I sat directly opposite him, and we started talking. He asked why I wanted to meet with him, and I told him that it was difficult to put into words but that somehow I knew that I was bound and I wanted liberation. I believed a much bigger experience of life than this was possible for a human being. As we talked, he began telling me things about myself as if he had an inside view. He told me a lot of very personal, specific, insightful things.

Then something very strange happened. While we were sitting there talking, Ram Dass no longer looked like Ram Dass. As I sat there watching him, he started to look completely different. Everything about the way he looked changed. His eyes, his face, his hair all kept changing. He took on many different forms, which looked like the embodiment of ancient wisdom and grace, which I perceived as manifestations of many various masters. It looked as if with every breath he was changing into a different enlightened being. His physical form actually changed. After some time, he asked me what was happening with me, and I can only imagine that I must have had a funny expression on my face. I said that nothing was happening; I was just watching his form change. He said, "Does that freak you out?" I said, "No; I can't believe this, yet somehow it seems more real than anything else that has ever happened to me." Not only is it strange to watch someone's form change and even disappear, but it's even stranger to find this so familiar and normal. It was as though what I refer to as myself was also the same self sitting in the chair across from me. I was in a presence that felt like home, that felt like me. This experience made me realize that our forms are so transient. I understood that our individual identities were transitory and that there was something absolutely stable within, which I longed to uncover.

The experience was powerful. It showed me that we all have the same inner self, which is just covered by our different personalities and who knows what else. After the meeting, I was elated. I thought that now I would have no difficulty uncovering what was truly me.

Of course, I did not feel comfortable telling many people about that experience. Most people would think I was simply a nutcase. One of my friends I did mention it to said it must have been an LSD flashback, but I had never had even one drug flashback before that, and I've had none since, so I knew that was not what it was. A New Age person that I knew told me that my third eye chakra had opened, but I was clueless about what had happened. I only knew that I was deeply struck by the experience and more than ever, I wanted more. Later, I visited Ram Dass at his home in Northern California and asked him if he was my guru. He said no, he was not a guru. He said that sometimes, when someone's seeking is intense, things happen through him. He said that when I met my real guru, I would know it. I thought my spiritual journey was off and running and that big things were going to happen to me. All that happened more than thirty years ago.

So, as we sat before the fire on our island that August evening, I told Sadhguru my Ram Dass story. "When I saw you for the first time," I said to Sadhguru, "you seemed to be the same being or the same essence I had seen so long ago with Ram Dass. It was all so familiar and all I could think was, uh-oh. I knew this gig was about to be up for me. What is real had finally shown back up."

Sadhguru then started to explain what happened. "Ram Dass, as you know, went to Neem Karoli Baba," he said. "Neem Karoli Baba was a phenomenal being of immense capabilities. He was a mystic, one who did not have the burden of education. I have to talk to you in your language and say things that you can understand according to your sensibilities.

"You see, Cheryl, how carefully I am going around with you? Neem Karoli Baba doesn't have to bother with all that. That is the freedom of being uneducated. So, out of his love for Ram Dass, or out of Ram Dass's own sincerity and willingness to receive, a certain dimension definitely descended upon him.

"I don't know whether Ram Dass said this only to you at a certain moment or if he said it to everybody, but in the very nature of things, Ram Dass cannot be your guru. However, he can be a good window to show you another dimension of life, which is exactly what he did. Because Ram Dass is not Ram Dass out of his own capabilities, Ram Dass is not Ram Dass out of his own *sadhana*. Ram Dass has become Ram Dass because in his life he did one sensible thing: He sat with a man like Neem Karoli Baba. He had the necessary sense to just sit there with him, and he imbibed a certain aspect of that being. Neem Karoli Baba wanted many windows to open, so he created one window and sent it to America."

Sadhguru then asked if I was familiar with Microsoft Windows. "I think you are using XP. You know that? So, this is like that. This is a certain kind of software, a window.

He opened a window and sent it to America so that you could see something. If you sat with him with a certain intensity and involvement, you would see things, but the window itself may not see it."

I wondered about that because I had later read where Ram Dass said that sometimes he isn't even there in meetings with people.

"Windows never see," Sadhguru said. "Our teachers are windows. They are capable of making people experience and see things way beyond their own capabilities. Windows only show. Now, they are not there as teachers. They are just there as windows to show people something they may not have seen. This is also the experience of many teachers. The Isha Yoga and Inner Engineering programs have become such powerful mediums of experience as the teachers are put through a grueling training process and, above all, a very intense *sadhana*, many of them for five to eight years. They learn to keep themselves aside. They just have to learn to be there in a certain state of absence; the rest will happen well beyond their own understanding and capabilities. They find that in their classes, many people are experiencing things that they themselves may not have seen. They are longing to experience those things. It may not have happened to them, but through them it is happening to so many people because through the window you can grasp the beauty of the Himalayas, but the window itself may not have grasped the beauty of the Himalayas.

"So, Ram Dass is a good window, not muddled with muck; a clean, glass window. It is good. It shows you many things and it is wonderful. It is wonderful of Ram Dass that he admits to you that he is not your guru. He is just a window. It is so wonderful. His humility is wonderful because most people in his position would immediately claim that, being a window, they are themselves the Himalayas. Ram Dass is a wonderful window because he knows his limitations. He knows the beauty of who he is and at the same time he knows the limitation of who he is. It is a beautiful thing when a human being knows his or her own limitations, when a human being is straight with themselves.

"I am not talking about limitations you have set for yourself as a matter of convenience. I am talking about the limitations that existence has put on you, which are not convenient. When you admit your limitations, it brings certain humility in you. It puts you where you belong. It is very important that you are always where you belong because whatever you imagine about yourself will not take you anywhere."

Then Sadhguru said, "Can I tell you a joke? You are talking about such serious things as a Swami changing forms, so I don't know if you are up for a joke."

"Yes," I said, "I am always up for a joke." I was just happy he didn't think I had been hallucinating. He took what I said seriously and helped me to understand what happened.

Sadhguru cheerfully began to tell us his joke. He likes jokes almost as much as he likes playing games.

"One day a pheasant and a bull were grazing in the field. The bull was grazing; the pheasant was picking out the ticks off the bull's body. They are used to each other, so it's going on as usual. Then the pheasant became nostalgic and said, 'When I was young, I could fly and sit on the topmost branch of the big tree out there, but now I can't even get to the first branch.' The bull said nonchalantly, 'Oh! What's the problem? Just eat my droppings and it will give you all the nourishment that you need to go to the topmost branch.' The pheasant said, 'Really? You mean just eating your droppings will get me to the top of the tree?' 'Yes, try and see!' he replied. So the pheasant hesitantly ate some droppings, and that very day he flew up to the first branch! Every day he ate more and more droppings. In about a fortnight's time, he reached the topmost branch. He sat there. The pheasant was so thrilled, having eaten the droppings and being able to sit on the topmost branch like when he was young. Now when the farmer, who was sitting on his balcony, saw this fat pheasant sitting on the topmost branch of the tree, he just could not ignore him. The farmer pulled out his shotgun and shot the pheasant off the tree! The moral of the story is: Bullshit may get you to the top, but it will never let you stay there."

After we all laughed, Sadhguru got serious again and continued explaining.

"So, whatever you think about yourself is irrelevant," he said. "You may tell yourself all kinds of stories about yourself. You may think all kinds of fancy things about yourself, but it has nothing to do with the existential reality. Your ideas and thoughts may have some social relevance, but the relevance ends there. The way existence holds you—I want you to understand—the very way you are existing right now, is perceived by life, and the life-making material you call God perceives you exactly as you are right now. The very space in the existence perceives you exactly as you are right now, not the way you wish you were, not the way you are dressed, not the way you look, not the way you speak, not the way you tell yourself you are, and not the way the world thinks about you. But, just the way you actually are is constantly perceived by the existence.

"You can deceive yourself, you can deceive your society, you can deceive the world around you, and you can deceive your friends, but this existence cannot be deceived. To try to deceive existence is to make a fool out of yourself. Everything you are is constantly perceived. You cannot get away with pretending anything. All deceptions are the product of the mind. Your fundamental existence is not of the mind. One way of describing what is spiritual is that it is beyond the process of the mind. Right now, all that you perceive through your sense perceptions goes through the process of the mind. Mind is make-believe. It is in this context that it is said that everything is Maya, or illusion."

As often happens while listening to Sadhguru answer a question I've asked, I fell into a deep stillness. I began to resonate with his answer, realizing it shed some light on a change that had taken place after the experience with Ram Dass (the experience I spoke with him about earlier). Sitting with Ram Dass, I really got the understanding that God is yourself, the same inner self that is always observing my life, that is in everyone and everything. We all have the same inner self. We have different personalities and egos, but our inner selves are the same. When that self spoke to me through Ram Dass I also felt totally bathed in love—and the love stripped me of all pretenses. I came to the realization that if there isn't anything about me that's not known, and I'm loved regardless, then what's there to hide? It was a very liberating thing, like all is forgiven because you're loved anyway. You are free to be yourself.

Thinking about Sadhguru's words, I was reminded of something else that happened during the trek I went on with him and a group of meditators in the Himalayas a couple of years ago. The most difficult part of the trek was at a place called Tapovan, which is at 14,600 feet above sea level and partly traverses a solid sheet of glacier. There was a woman there with a daunting presence; remarkably, she had on a perfectly pressed sari, the sort of Indian dress a woman would wear in a city. The sari's perfection looked out of place, to say the least, on top of an icy mountain. The woman was very kind, warm, and hospitable. We were told that she is known as Bengali Ma, which means she is from Bengal in India. Ma means a motherly figure. She lives in a dwelling of which part is a natural cave. It seems that many people visit her there on the mountain, and she is well known in that area and revered as a mystic.

Some of the meditators from our group went to see her at her dwelling and offered their respects. She asked where they had come from; they explained that they were from South India and were with their guru, Sadhguru. Then she inquired, "Who is Sadhguru?" One of the meditators showed her his picture, and she studied it for a while before saying, "He is not here anymore! He finished his work and left long ago. He is no longer here."

This totally unnerved the people in our group. In fact, something about her had already shaken them. There was something so powerful about her presence that two from our group burst into tears as soon as they first approached her. When they insisted that Sadhguru had come here with us, she just smiled and again said, "No. He has left long ago."

I asked Sadhguru about this incident. I was curious to know what the woman might have seen by looking at Sadhguru's picture. She, too, seemed to have a totally different level of perception from ordinary people.

Sadhguru again laughed and said, "See, some people cannot be deceived. All this deception I created, I deceived all you. Now someone goes to Bengali Ma, and she says, 'He should not be here.' She said this because only life in a certain level of vibrancy and karmic appendages is accounted by the existence as life. I am not an account. That is what she meant. As you know, I was programmed to leave immediately after the consecration of the Dhyanalinga, which was finally coming to fruition after three lifetimes of intense effort. In many ways, I as an individual life, was absorbed by the existence, but by tying myself initially to a variety of life around me and later to more specific life, I have continued an apparition like existence—but, see, I am for 'real,' Cheryl!

"All this may sound too far-fetched and difficult to believe, but now you must see that what the modern scientists are talking about is as much beyond logic as mysticism is. Do you know that they are talking about eleven different parallel existences right here as you and I sit on this island? In the yogic systems, we have been talking about twenty-one different dimensions of existence. So, this Bengali Ma said this not because she knows anything, but simply because she is just existence. She is not a woman, she is not a man, she is not a saint, and she is not a sage or a god. She is simply existence, so she has a certain uncluttered perception. I feel quite silly that this woman in the Himalayas is able to see through all this.

"If you keep your window clear, you simply see things the way they are. She is not the lowest or the highest. She simply is, and this is most important. High and low is all made up; these ideas have nothing to do with reality. Your sense of high and low, good and bad, virtue and sin, God and the devil, are all your own creation and your own projections. These projections have nothing to do with reality. Reality is just this. How you are with this is all there is."

Sadhguru continued, "Ram Dass may not know it, but he is a clean window. You could use him to see many things, but still he cannot be your guru simply because he has no methods. If you have spent sufficient time with him—I don't know how much time you have spent with him—probably he will go on talking about the same thing. Nothing happens. If you simply sit with him, something can happen. But, nothing can happen as a result of his teachings because he is not equipped to be a guru. He is a clean window. He is a means for a clear view.

"You must just look through the window. You must not carry the window with you. You don't have to carry the window with you for it to show you things. A clean window shows you things. That's all there is to it. Now, this could do many things for you, but still these glimpses are only to inspire you. A glimpse in itself does not get you anywhere. A glimpse in itself does not transform you. You saw other masters, or whatever you saw, and it only inspires you to seek. It is not a destination, and it is wonderful of Ram Dass to remind you that he is not the destination for you. There are many windows like this, particularly in India. Many, many windows like this."

"Sadhguru, how is a guru different from a window?" I asked.

"Generally, a guru will not give you glimpses of the sort that you are telling me about unless he sees a particular need to break through a specific limitation in a person. Instead, he will give you methods that will slowly wear out your limited nature. These methods will help you evolve out of where you are right now. Because glimpses are just exuberant experiences, they are not of much use to you. You may like them, but often they can fuel your imagination or even lead you to hallucinatory states. You see, there is always the danger of the mind distorting everything as per your needs and requirements, causing further limitations. This danger is constantly lurking.

"Probably you will understand it better this way. A guru is like a technologist or a mechanic who will give you the necessary tools and guidance as to how to fix your existing faculties so you can become a vehicle for your ultimate blossoming. This is a subjective technology that cannot be grasped objectively, hence all the mystery."

I said, "But it is still mysterious. How is it that you can see what we need? I have not been inspired for years. Though I have done a fair amount of spiritual practices, I never felt they took me anywhere."

He said, "Cheryl, is it really that difficult to believe that someone could have a different level of perception? Even your dogs can perceive things you cannot perceive. If I close my eyes and sit here and someone walks into the room, even with my eyes closed I can tell you what kind of person walked in. Even your dogs can do that. Take this tree right here for example. You see this tree, how it's being blocked by the branches of this bigger tree? It's very obvious to all us that if we want the smaller tree to grow, then we have to cut off these branches that are blocking it. It's just in that context that I can see what needs to happen for a person.

"Many teachers have taught you proper yoga with correct methods, but the subjective dimension was not there. Even though some things happened, a steady process toward your spiritual well-being did not happen. The teachers came from good stables, so the methods were correct, but the subjective dimension was missing. We in the yogic culture treat a spiritual process or yogic method as a live deity. This is because a method itself may create some physical benefits and mental stability, but it will not take you beyond that. The one who transmits it should be able to infuse life into it. For the deep dimensions to open within you, it must be infused with life. I mentioned Patanjali to you earlier. Patanjali is the father of yoga and the yoga sutras. The word sutra, when assimilated by him, means a thread that gives a realized being the freedom to make a garland out of it. Although, without the thread there is no garland; you do not wear a garland for its thread.

"Depending upon a certain master's accomplishment, he adds flowers or beads or diamonds to the sutra using this basic thread. If you just wear the thread, it is not of any great consequence. It is just wasted in ignorance. The reason we want to dissolve the way you are right now is so you don't get in the way of the transmission that is well beyond you.

"Cheryl, if you lack inspiration, someone or something can inspire you—but the purpose of the inspiration ends there. If you want information, you can get information, but knowing will never happen to you. You must understand that life exists in many different dimensions. When we are in a certain dimension of experience, another dimension, whatever it may be, is not a reality for us. For example, for you when the sun comes up in the morning, it is light. When the sun goes down in the evening, there is darkness. This is reality for you. There are many animals—let us say the owl—for him, if the sun comes up in the morning, there is darkness. When the sun goes down in the evening, it is light.

"If you and this owl sit together and start arguing about which is light and which is darkness, you will not get anywhere. You know it will get you nowhere because your perception is in two different dimensions. The sensory instruments of perception only cater to your survival. It is a poor way to live if you cannot see that life is happening in many other ways besides the way you know it. That will not take you anywhere. So, when we are talking about yoga beyond the physical and mental well-being, we are talking about breaking the limitations of this dimension and moving into a totally different dimension of life: from the physical world to another existence by itself. This other existence is not somewhere else, but it is not available to a person when he is totally rooted in his physical nature.

"If you want to seek another dimension, it is always best that you have a person who is already in that other dimension. Otherwise, it looks like an endless journey. There are a few people who are willing to set sail into an open ocean, not knowing where they are going. They simply go, and some day they may find something. A few may find something. Some will just die, but a few will get across. Now, today you know that the world is round, and if you go this amount of distance, eventually you will hit land. Suppose you did not know all this. You take one boat and you go off into the ocean. You simply keep going. That takes a certain kind of person. Not everyone can do it. Not everyone can make this journey. You have to be willing to throw your life into it.

"So, if you wish to walk into a dimension that is not in your present level of experience and understanding, there are a few ways in which you can enter it. One way is that I give you the road map and you find your own way. It is entirely up to you. So, when you are trying to go into a dimension that is beyond your experience and understanding, a road map is good but you know that even with a road map you can be lost all the time. Another way is that I put on my taillights and say, 'Just follow me.' Now you try to keep up at a certain pace. Suddenly the fog comes and you can't see the taillights, and suddenly you think you have been ditched. Then you see a glimmer of the taillights and you think, 'Oh, it's still okay.' This keeps happening. You keep getting lost and question if you are being ditched. There may be ten cars between you and me and again you think, 'Oh, he left me.' That is how most people are following. Another way you can get there is you just sit on my bus. Once you get on my bus, even if you doze off, it does not matter. You will get to the destination, but you cannot do the driving. So, these are the three ways. I am game for any of them. If you are an adventurous kind, use the road map. If you do not necessarily want adventure, but you want to act brave, then we will keep the taillights on. Most people who claim to be adventurous avoid adventure every chance they get. Just look carefully. Or, if you are tired of getting lost here and you don't have anything to prove to yourself or anybody else, you just get on the bus and plonk yourself down. It will go where it has to go. You choose. Whichever way is fine with me. If you have lots of time, then play around with the road map. If you are in a hurry then just hop on the bus.

"Now, this is neither easy nor difficult. It is just simple. It is so simple that your mind—which is being pulled and pushed by so many factors, which is functioning within the limitations that you have gathered, where you have made your limitations gold plated—is just getting confused. If you stop gold plating your limitations, if you stop seeing your shackles as ornaments that you wear and are proud of, then it is very simple and you are on full-time. Please see how many deceptive ways you seek support for your limitations from the people around you. You want approval for your limitations. You want these hindrances to be thought of as all right."

I was taken aback by this. Of course, he was right. I looked over at Leela, who was smiling at me. The light from the fire danced across her face. I leaned back against a tree and thought of all the limitations I had placed on myself over the years. Why we do that to ourselves, I wondered. The fire crackled and drew my attention back to Sadhguru. His eyes were as deep as two wells.

I thought about how interesting it is that we unconsciously fix our identity. I had not realized how we ourselves limit our identities whenever we say, "I'm this way or I'm that way; this is the kind of person I am." There was a lot of talk around about having no boundaries, and I didn't know what that meant. But now I understood better what people meant and realized that, if anything, for a long time I had been making my boundaries smaller. Prior to meeting Sadhguru, I can see that what I was comfortable with was shrinking: I had gotten more particular about what I liked and didn't like, and quicker to judge if I thought something wasn't measuring up. For instance, if a place didn't have air conditioning, you could definitely count me out. To go for a walk, it had to be seventy degrees and sunny. I was accepting all this as normal. I know I had accepted many of my limitations as normal. This is definitely not true anymore. Now, there are so many things I'm less likely to avoid. And, even if I do have resistance at the time, afterwards, I'm always glad I did it.

This brought up another question I wanted Sadhguru to answer, so I asked, "Sadhguru, many people I know think that they are fine just the way they are. In fact, some even take it to the point, in this country, of thinking that either they have everything all figured out or they 'have arrived' or made it. If they think they are already there, how is any transformation possible?"

"The problem is, Cheryl, that whatever you polish will shine. This is so with ignorance, too. I see this trend today in the world, especially in the West, that instead of admitting what you do not know, people are assuming realities that are not yet in their experience. Knowing existential realities intellectually does not mean anything. There was a time when people believed God was up there. Now there are many people going about saying 'God is everywhere.' There are some who say, 'God is within me.' In a way, all these statements are equally flaky. Sometimes people, through various means, have had certain elevating experiences. This they are even calling enlightenment. You can have elevating experiences by doing almost anything with certain intensity. This is like you are on this side of the wall and you got on your trampoline and jumped hard and you got to glimpse what is on the other side of the wall. Just having a glimpse of what is beyond is not it. Finding ways to cross the wall is the ultimate goal of the spiritual process.

"Right now the situation is that if someone has no need for antidepressants, he thinks he has arrived. A little bit of peace and well-being is not the ultimate goal.

The ultimate is not about well-being at all, but you cannot approach it unless you are sitting on the stable ground of well-being. Just having physical well-being is like making a journey in a stationary car.

"If you just sit in the parking lot in your dream car, morning becomes noon, noon becomes evening, evening becomes night, and night becomes day again. Seasons will change, flowers will bloom, and leaves will fall. You can sit right there and believe that you are going somewhere because the scenery has been changing. To know well-being, you don't need any spiritual process. Keeping yourself well exercised, reading a good book, maintaining good relationships, and maybe playing golf should take care of your well-being. The spiritual process becomes relevant to you only when you realize that, though physical and mental well-being settles many things in your life, it is only a platform to fulfill the deeper longings within you. There is something within you that is constantly longing for boundless expansion. When you start a spiritual process, physical and mental well-being happen naturally. It is more of a side benefit, not the purpose. So, when this little benefit happens to people, a lot of them like to assume they have arrived."

I again found myself slipping into silence. The other evenings during our week were filled with many periods of silence, but since I was running out of time and still had lots more questions, I wanted to ask Sadhguru about something else that was eating at me. I had a recent experience of him making a reference to something about my past that he would have had no way of knowing anything about. I was eager to get to the bottom of how he had known that particular thing since I had not mentioned it to him or anyone else. I said, "So, Sadhguru, you seem to be able to see what is going on with us, and you are always teasing us that now that we have made the mistake of sitting in front of you, we no longer have any secrets. But can you actually see our past or what is going on with us?" I asked.

Sadhguru said, "If I couldn't, I could not do this kind of work."

"But what does that really mean?" I asked, still probing for some understanding.

Sadhguru slowly explained, "The first thing I do when I see a person is bow down. I touch their innermost core and recognize them as an embodiment of the divine. That is why the bowing down. Next, I see the heap of impressions that one has gathered. I see all the karmic structure and the resultant tendencies. With some people, there are very strong impressions of past events. Though they are of the past, they have become a living reality within them, and of course then there is the clear possibility of where these tendencies may take that person if he continues his life within the compulsions of these tendencies. You mentioned before that you noticed I often answer a different question than that which is asked. Someone may ask a wrong question, but I must give them a right answer. Sometimes when someone asks one type of question, I will start talking about a completely different aspect because I don't listen to their words; I listen to them as individuals. I listen to them as reverberations of their accumulated impressions or, shall I say, right now I see you as just an accumulation of your karma. So, it is true that once you have made the mistake of sitting with me, there is no such thing as privacy in your life. When there is love, there is no need for privacy. Those whom you truly love you always take into your private spaces. As I have enveloped all beings in absolute love, I don't allow them any privacy."

Sadhguru started laughing uproariously and then got up, walked to the shoreline, and dove into the water for an impromptu swim. As we heard the water splash, Leela and I made eye contact. I'm sure we were both thinking the same thing: We don't have any towels or dry clothes for him. You really have to be prepared for anything around him!

Much later, after we finished off a bag of chips and salsa, I remembered to ask Sadhguru about the America poem.

Not surprisingly, Sadhguru was quiet for a time before he said, "The last time I was at Center Hill Lake,

I met a Native American man there. That is why I wrote the poem."

"Why did meeting that man inspire you to write that poem?" I asked.

Sadhguru astonished me by saying, "The man I met had been standing perfectly still in the same spot for the last three hundred years."

"Three hundred years, Sadhguru?" I asked

Sadhguru said, "You know how the Native American Indians are portrayed as very proud and always fit, strong people. They knew fighting. They were good warriors, had great pride in their culture, and were very straight. They would fight a battle with you today and tomorrow, if you as much as called him a brother, they would be just fine. That is how they were. For them, killing and dying in a battle was an honor. They never knew that somebody could come and own the land, take it away. They just did not understand. They saw the earth as a live force that sustained them. This is one of the few cultures in the world that did not look up when you said God. They looked to the earth as the force that created and nurtured them.

"When I happened to be walking in a certain part of the Appalachian Forest in Tennessee, I saw a man standing still. He was standing still, frozen in a certain position of despair and shame. I saw that he was in that, you know, the past regalia of the native tribes. He was just standing there completely frozen in full regalia. Whenever I see someone in extreme movement or they are immediately still, I put myself into it because both of these situations are possibilities for me to do something. The in-between, medium movement doesn't mean much. People in extreme movement, they are a possibility. People who are utterly still, they too are a possibility. I cannot keep myself away from these two kinds of people because that is a field of possibilities.

"So, then I saw that it was almost three hundred years, close to three hundred years, that he was standing there frozen. I saw that the situation behind his life was that this particular person had the responsibility and the privilege of protecting his elder brother, who was a certain kind of leader or chief of the community. He was like a right-hand man to him. He was his assistant, protecting him in every way. Now in that tradition, elder brother does not necessarily mean that he was born from the same father or mother. You can take up brothers in the same way that you can take up friends. This man held this elder brother in great esteem, and he held it as a great privilege to walk by his side and protect him. A situation happened where he had set up a meeting for the chief with some military people. Somehow this chief was deceived and this elder brother, who was of a certain leadership and prominence, was killed by the white man. This man felt so responsible. This man that I came across stood there in absolute despair, failure, distress, and shame. Such extreme emotions were within him that he had just been standing there for three hundred years. When I saw him, he was still standing right there. Not in a physical body; obviously the earth fell back to earth, but the rest of him stood there just as he was in that moment. So, I thought, it is time he moves on. Too much time in shame, too much time in defeat is not good. I helped him to move on from that situation. And, I wrote one bad poem after that."

AMERICA

The brooding darkness of these woods
Fed upon the native blood
In the twisted tangle of the fallen wood
The spirit of the fallen Indian stood

Oh brothers, your identity a mistake
Those who oceans crossed did make
The greed for gold and land
Laid waste the spirit of wisdom and grace

The children of those who by murder did take
Are taintless of their forefather's mistake
But those who lived, fed upon milk of courage and pride
Stand as spirits of defeat and shame

O the murdered and the murderous
Embrace me, let me set your spirits to rest

There was nothing to say. I was strongly affected by the poem and the image of the Indian, the absolute horror of that kind of shame. I felt immobile just hearing about it: a person who was so distraught that he became frozen in time, so to speak. How could this be? What a bone-chilling, stomach-wrenching story. A story like this would have been totally unbelievable to me before I knew Sadhguru; instead, I was tearing up over the terrible experience that poor man went through.

Maybe I had completely taken leave of my sensibilities, but nothing that Sadhguru spoke about seemed unimaginable to me. It just seems matter of fact. After having spent so much time with him, everything often appears to be supported by a magical field of energy. This happens so frequently when I am with him that now, even if something is not in my present level of experience, I am open to the possibility. It is more along the lines of how inconceivable a fax machine or the Internet once was. Very little seems difficult to imagine. If you had known what a hardcore skeptic, bordering on a cynic, that I used to be, you would know that this change in my thinking is completely out of character. If anyone else I know other than Sadhguru spoke of these things, I would just think they were crazy and would have nothing to do with them. I have experienced Sadhguru as a mystic, and I no longer doubt that he has a bigger sphere of perception than anyone else I have ever known.

The more time I spend with him, the more extraordinary things I witness firsthand. I was working on a project for Isha a few months ago, and I had a meeting with Sadhguru in Nashville, Tennessee. I got to the meeting early and Leela told me about a pilot for a television show that Sadhguru had been on the previous day. Sadhguru was one of three people on a panel to answer questions about life and life's mysteries. He was there with an American shaman and a psychiatrist from a prominent university.

A woman approached the panel with a taped video of her husband. Her husband was in his forties and was diagnosed with terminal cancer. He was at the end stage of the cancer and was rapidly approaching death. The woman showed a very moving video of her husband in bed on life-support. He was asking questions, pertinent questions, about death and what was going to happen to him. He talked about prayer and asked why God should save him. People had been telling him to pray. All his life he had been praying, but now he was not so sure. Why would God respond to him? Why not the people in Iraq and so many others who are suffering in the world? The three people on the panel were all supposed to approach his questions from their own perspectives. The shaman went on about there being some kind of wonderful party on the other side, where all his old friends and loved ones would be waiting for him. Sadhguru responded to this man's genuine longing to know, at the final stage of his life, with a different level of vision and compassion. Once he started speaking, he seemed to take over the show.

As Leela was telling me the story, Sadhguru came out and joined our conversation. He said that the two other people on the show were doing their best to give this man solace. He went on to say that the man was not looking for solace; he was looking for help and understanding. Sadhguru offered his help to the man's wife. Sadhguru went on to say that the woman called back to say that her husband did want his help. Sadhguru then said that in an hour we would be going to go to his house so he could help him.

As I was listening to Sadhguru, his words slowly started to sink in. "We are going to the house of this man who was on the videotape on that show yesterday in one hour?" I asked, thinking I had not understood what Sadhguru was telling me.

"Yes, he wants my help," he answered.

"You're going to help him?" I asked incredulously. "What does that mean? You are going to help him die?"

"Yes," Sadhguru said. "He and his wife are very brave."

"Well Sadhguru, what does that mean? Will he get enlightened?" I asked.

Sadhguru laughed at me and said, "No; he will not get what you want, but he will have a very soft landing."

I still did not have any idea what Sadhguru was talking about, but the next thing I knew Sadhguru, Leela, and I were on our way to this man's home. In the car on the way there I said, "Sadhguru, you know that Doctor Kevorkian got in a lot of trouble for helping people die. In fact, I think he is in prison now."

Sadhguru laughed loud and said, "Cheryl, I am not going there to kill him. I am not going to pull off his life-support. I am not even going to touch him. I am just going to help make his exit smooth and easy."

About thirty minutes later, we arrived at their home. It was a small house in a modest neighborhood. When we got there, the house was filled with people, primarily family members. I had heard Sadhguru speak about death at one of the *sathsangs* I attended, and I remembered that he said it is actually easier for us to die if we are not surrounded by our family. He said it is easier to let go when we are away from our loved ones and our attachments. That is obviously not how we do things in this country. For some reason, we all feel that we should be there at the exact moment our loved ones depart.

After we met the man's family and they thanked Sadhguru for coming, we were led into the bedroom, where he slept. He was in bed without a shirt on and was covered with a blanket that was folded under his arms.

He was hooked up to several IVs. When Sadhguru walked into the room, the man's eyes popped open. He actually looked good. I had heard he was in incredible pain, so I was surprised that he looked so awake and not like he was in pain or even suffering at all. Sadhguru just stood there with his eyes closed for some time then he hugged the man and left.

On the ride back Sadhguru said, "I fixed it. He will leave tomorrow. It is a full moon. It is an auspicious day, and a very good time to leave."

"What do you mean you fixed it?" I asked. "How can you know he will actually leave tomorrow? Doctors can never predict things that closely."

"I am not guessing about this, Cheryl," he replied. "His life energies have become very feeble and have gone beyond the point of having the capacity to hold on to the body for very long, no matter what. With of all these life-support mechanisms, they may be able to push his life for maybe a week or two, but in the process he will most probably become totally unconscious and lose the opportunity to leave this life in awareness. So, I have set up his energies in such a way that he will leave at the beginning of the full moon tomorrow between eleven thirty and two o'clock. It is a very good day to leave."

The following day, I was back at the flat where Sadhguru was staying. About an hour after I arrived, around one o'clock, the phone rang. Sadhguru received word that the man had just passed. They told Sadhguru that from the time he went to see him, all the pain seemed to have stopped. Being present for that was quite an experience. I had not had any other opportunity to ask Sadhguru more about that when it happened, but since Leela and I had him captive on the island again, I thought he might talk about it some more. I asked what he meant when he said that he helped that man to have "a soft landing."

"The transition was definitely smooth as I dismantled the residual karmic structure, as he is still young and that would allow that life to find a form very soon," he said.

Taking that to mean he would reincarnate right away I asked, "So, being born again quickly is a good thing?" Obviously, I was clueless about all this. I think I still harbored some slim hope that once I died I would be enlightened, or at least understand a lot more than I do now.

"Definitely," Sadhguru said. "It is a very good thing."

"So, what is good about it?" I asked.

"Cheryl, when you are in a human body, you can do so much more to evolve yourself."

"Are we still evolving when we are not having a physical birth?" I asked.

"Yes, but things happen much more slowly. Human birth is a huge opportunity. Something that may take a year here could take a hundred times longer there."

I did not really understand, but I was beginning to see why a lot of the Eastern traditions talked about the importance of a human birth and also the importance of the moment of death. I asked Sadhguru why the moment of death was said to be important.

Sadhguru answered, "When one leaves his body in awareness consciously, he can easily set the future course for the life within. One who can witness this moment of transition gets to glimpse and perceive life in ways that might not otherwise be available to him. As this transition is like a twilight zone, you get to view it being away from both life and death. The various yogic practices are designed and structured to bring about this profound glimpse. It is for this purpose that in many cultures of the world the last moment of life or the moment of death is considered very important."

Sadhguru's assertion that we had not yet understood the enormity of being human was making more sense now. He often said that many humans are primarily focused on survival—what to eat, where to sleep, having sex, and so on—but humans, unlike animals, have the capacity to reach the peak of consciousness. I had often felt that I had not made the most of my life, and I had wasted a lot of it. In fact, when I met Sadhguru, he said that I was in danger of wasting the rest of my life to laziness and complacency. I didn't disagree with him. In fact, that was my primary concern: Why had I not been able to do more with myself? I was enjoying life to a certain extent, but I was never without the longing for something more than just this small, ordinary experience of life.

"Sadhguru," I said, "I have heard you say on many occasions that most people don't want truth. They just want solace. I take that to mean that they just want to keep their belief systems intact to keep themselves comfortable. I've also heard you repeatedly refuse to talk about things outside of people's experience, but isn't it more useful to understand how things really work? If this human life is such a huge opportunity for us to evolve, isn't it better to know that than to sit around waiting for everything to get fixed after we die? If reincarnation is what happens, will you explain more about it to us? Once we have a human birth, do we just somehow keep creating a story until eventually something in us wants out?"

Just as I finished asking my question, a localized storm appeared out of nowhere with loud thunder and bright lightning. As much as I hated for it to happen, the weather brought our wonderful night to a brisk end. When I glanced at my watch, it was already close to five o'clock. The rest of my questions were going to have to wait. I hated to see this night end. I wished it could have lasted forever. Not only was this night ending, my week of midnights was also coming to a close.

It was an ending, and yet I knew it was also a beginning.

EPILOGUE

The next morning and the end of our time at the lake came around way too quickly, at warp speed. After a light breakfast, Sadhguru, Leela, and I packed our things and loaded up the cars to head out in three different directions. Leela was going back to her home in the Midwest. Sadhguru and I were heading back to the airport, where Sadhguru was catching a plane to California and I was departing to Florida to visit my parents.

After a tearful goodbye to Leela, I locked up the house and Sadhguru and I left for Atlanta, with him driving of course. During this ride, I was much quieter than on the first trip, soaking in all that I had experienced during that incredible week. I could scarcely believe that so much could happen to me in such a short period of time.

More happened to me in a week with this glorious being than in the whole thirty-plus years before meeting Sadhguru, which I had spent trying to find understanding and some kind of inner experience. Yet, I know I have barely scratched the surface of who Sadhguru is and who I can become or what is possible for a person.

Because of Sadhguru, a dimension is opening up in me that was not accessible before. This has completely changed how I experience life. I certainly still do not have all the answers I have been looking for, nor have I suddenly become enlightened, but something is definitely happening within me.

When I asked Sadhguru why everything was so intense now and why this yoga worked so much better than anything else I'd tried, he said, "Because I do not teach yoga. I am yoga." When I asked him again at a later time, he said, "Because it is a live transmission." I don't know what that means, but I feel that it is more than just the physical aspects of the practice that are working on me. I can't believe that there was a time when I questioned the value of having a guru.

The same is now true for me as it was for the young man who first told me about Sadhguru that day in the airport: "All this has had a liberating effect on my attachments and fears." I am now cruising at a much higher altitude than before, regardless of external situations. This does not mean that things do not still fall apart from time to time. They do, but I am no longer consumed with worry when things are challenging. I definitely am not worrying ahead on spec like I used to. Mark Twain once said, "I have been through terrible things in my life, some of which actually happened." Instead of a life ruled by outside circumstances, I am very steady and happy, even if things become challenging.

Sadhguru said that once you are a yogi, nothing bad can ever happen to you again because there is nothing that you cannot use for your ultimate growth. Even in hell a yogi can be happy. If you are happy, there is no such thing as hell.

When I look back and see how much has changed in the several years since meeting Sadhguru and beginning the yoga processes, it seems like a miracle. Sadhguru says that miracles do not happen with a bang; instead, they happen quietly. They happen as quietly as flowers bloom and trees grow.

As I was sitting back, enjoying the ride to the airport and absorbed in my thoughts, Sadhguru asked me if I was going to go on the trip to Mount Kailash in Tibet, to which he would soon be taking a group of people. He mentioned it the previous year, when I was in the

Himalayas with him and a bunch of other Isha meditators. He spoke about Mount Kailash and a place called Lake Mansarovar that he was interested in visiting. He told us what he knew about it at that time and asked who might want to go. Before I could think it through, my hand immediately shot up. I was dying to go.

When I got home, however, I did some research. It turns out that Mount Kailash soars up to twenty-two thousand feet. Just to get to the base of the mountain, one has to trek up to eighteen thousand feet, an altitude that is no simple trip. I discovered that the trip up the mountain was an extremely arduous journey and that many of those who embark upon it die every year. I also talked to a physician I know, who told me of two of her colleagues who went on a similar trip to Kailash with a small group of only fourteen people. They both died of pulmonary problems on the trip. I went from dying to go to thinking I would die if I did go. The website that I found also went on about altitude sickness and harsh, rapidly changing inclement weather, including landslides. Kailash is said to be the most difficult pilgrimage in Asia. Knowing Sadhguru, none of this came as any big surprise to me—not only that he would want to go there, but that it would be beyond challenging for me. I concluded that this trip was definitely not for me. Maybe if I were younger and more physically fit I would go.

So, there we were riding down the road when Sadhguru wanted to know if I was planning on going.

I replied, "No, I don't think so."

Sadhguru asked, "Why not, Cheryl? You should go. It would be good if you go."

He caught me off guard. I had really given it a lot of thought and was quite comfortable in my decision to pass, because I was convinced it would be way too difficult and uncomfortable for me. But I had not expected to be talking to him about it. It would be good for me to go? Sadhguru saying "it would be good if you go" is no light matter. I started to have this sinking feeling, filled with enormous trepidation that I was going to be taking this trip no matter how difficult it would be. So I said, "The thing is, Sadhguru, I would really love to go if it would not kill me, but I think it is really over my head given my age, fitness level, and all other things considered."

Sadhguru started laughing uproariously and said "Cheryl, if it does not kill you, it is not worth doing! Only if you are killed will you truly come alive. Let's do the killing in the most exotic place on the planet."

I did make the journey, but that's another story. . . .

THE ONE THAT IS

The flesh
The spirit
Only the means
To know
The one that is
—Sadhguru

APPENDIX ONE
Isha Yoga Programs

Gleaned from the core of the ancient yogic science and unveiled for every human being, Isha Yoga programs allow individuals to take tangible steps toward their inner growth. Designed by Sadhguru, the programs provide a rare opportunity for self-discovery under the guidance of a realized yogi.

At Isha, yoga is taught in its full depth and dimension and is communicated on an experiential level. The programs provide methods for establishing oneself in wholeness and vitality as the first stepping stone toward spiritual growth. The simple yet powerful practices taught in the basic Isha Yoga programs pave the path for inner exploration and self-transformation.

Tailored to suit individuals from every social and cultural background, Isha Yoga programs involve simple postures, meditation, and other powerful ways of transforming one's energies. They do not require physical agility or any previous knowledge or experience of yoga.

BASIC PROGRAMS
Inner Engineering

Inner Engineering is the basic Isha Yoga program, which is offered in many cities in the United States. In this intensive seven-day program, the foundation for exploring higher dimensions of life is established by offering tools that enable one to re-engineer one's self through the inner science of yoga. Once given the tools to rejuvenate themselves, people can optimize all aspects of health, inner growth, and success. For those seeking professional and personal excellence, this program offers keys for meaningful and fulfilling relationships at work, home, community, and most importantly, within one's self. The program also offers the tools necessary to create the balance between the challenges of a hectic career and the inner longing for peace and well-being.

The approach is a modern antidote to stress and presents simple but powerful processes from yogic science to purify the system and increase health and inner well-being. Program components include transmission of the sacred Shambhavi Maha Mudra as well as guided meditations.

When practiced on a regular basis, these tools have the potential to enhance one's experience of life on many levels.

Wholeness

Wholeness is an eight-day residential program conducted by Sadhguru at the Isha Yoga Center in India. It is scientifically structured to produce an environment conducive for personal exploration and transformation. The approach in this program is truly holistic, as it treats each person as a whole, recognizing the essential unity of body, mind, and spirit.

Practices learned in the Wholeness Program place great emphasis on purifying processes that renew the body's potency and act as a stress reducer and a preventative for disease. The practices taught at the Wholeness Program activate a subtle process that leads to a change in one's inner chemistry. Science today has proven that all physical and emotional states have a biological/chemical basis. The goal of the Wholeness Program is to transform a person's inner chemistry, which leads to physical health, joyfulness, and vitality, and which ultimately cultivates the person for the experience of a higher spiritual dimension.

This program features Shakti Chalana *kriya*, a series of powerful and purifying breathing techniques; *asanas,* dynamic yoga postures; and Shoonya meditation, an effortless process of conscious non-doing that stimulates the release of all physical, mental, and emotional blocks and that activates spontaneous expression of one's vital energy.

ADVANCED PROGRAMS
Bhava Spandana Program

Bhava Spandana Program (BSP) is a four-day, three-night residential program offered to those who have completed either the Inner Engineering or the Wholeness Program. This advanced meditation program is designed by Sadhguru to provide the opportunity to experience higher levels of consciousness beyond the limitations of the body and the mind. BSP offers the experience of a world of limitless love and joy.

According to Sadhguru, Isha Yoga programs prepare the mind and cultivate one's body and energy to look beyond one's physical reality. The process of yoga is to cultivate one's energies in such a way that gradually it breaks the physical limitations and one experiences life beyond the physical dimension. This is just a preparation so that when the energy begins to move, the mind doesn't resist. The practices slowly elevate one in this way.

Bhava Spandana is a boosting experience in the same direction. It is like making a person jump and look beyond the wall. "He sees beyond his limitation experientially. Once he sees that, he knows that one day he must go over the wall to see what is on the other side."

Samyama

Samyama is an intensive, eight-day residential program conducted by Sadhguru at the Isha Yoga Center in India. Samyama meditations provide the experiential possibility to free one from the bonds of karma and to purify the body and the mind to receive higher levels of energy. Samyama presents the potential for participants to reach heightened levels of consciousness and to experience explosive states of meditativeness in the presence of a self-realized yogi.

OTHER PROGRAMS
Hata Yoga

Hata Yoga, a two- to three-day residential program at Isha Yoga, is an opportunity to learn *surya namaskar* (sun salutation) along with a series of *asanas* (yoga postures). The program does not require any previous experience in yoga or particular physical agility. Participants need not have gone through any previous Isha Yoga programs. In this one-time program, the postures are imparted in such depth and precision that the one who goes through the program is enabled to practice them at home. Isha Hata Yoga is far beyond being a mere physical exercise, simply bending the body. This comprehensive set of *asanas* is scientifically designed in such a way that through regular practice, one can attain to a certain mastery over the body and the mind. Isha Hata Yoga not only improves health and well-being, it also brings the necessary balance within oneself to experience higher levels of energy. As a preparatory step for other Isha Yoga practices, it significantly enhances the experience of *kriyas* and meditation.

Isha Yoga for Children

Isha Yoga for Children offers a unique possibility for every child to experience a joyful blossoming of their natural potential. Isha Yoga celebrates the natural gifts within every child, including their sense of wonder and oneness with life.

The program introduces children to yoga through playful and joyful exploration, allowing each child to develop and live in optimal health and inner peace.

Isha Yoga for Children consists of an introduction to simple yoga practices, including Shakti Chalana *kriya* and *asanas,* as well as the cultivation of a deep sense of responsibility and reverence for life. The program content is presented through fun games and play so that children experience a sense of belonging and unity with life.

Participants of Isha Yoga for Children often experience enhanced concentration and memory, more focus, and improved mind-body coordination. The practices learned are an effective preventative for obesity, asthma, sinusitis, and other chronic ailments.

APPENDIX TWO
Isha Foundation

Isha Foundation is a nonreligious, nonprofit, public service organization that addresses all aspects of human well-being. From its powerful programs for inner transformation to its inspiring projects for society and environment, Isha activities are designed to create an inclusive culture that is the basis for global harmony and progress. This approach has gained worldwide recognition and is reflected in Isha Foundation's Special Consultative Status with the Economic and Social Council (ECOSOC) of the United Nations.

Supported by hundreds and thousands of active and dedicated volunteers in more than two hundred centers worldwide, the foundation's activities serve as a thriving model for human empowerment and community revitalization throughout the world.

ISHA YOGA CENTER

Isha Yoga Center, founded under the aegis of Isha Foundation, is located on 150 acres of lush land at the foothills of the Vellingiri Mountains, which are part of a reserve forest with abundant wildlife. Created as a powerful *sthana* (a center for inner growth), this popular destination attracts people from all parts of the world. It is unique in its offering of all aspects of yoga—*gnana* (knowledge), *karma* (action), *kriya* (energy), and *bhakthi* (devotion), and it revives the *guru-shishya parmapara* (traditional method of knowledge transfer from master to disciple).

The center houses the architecturally distinctive Spanda Hall, a sixty-four-thousand-square-foot meditation hall and program facility that is the venue of many advanced residential programs. Also located at the center are the Dhyanalinga Yogic Temple, Theerthakund, Isha Rejuvenation Center, Isha Home School, Nalanda (a corporate conference center), and Vanaprastha for families. Isha Yoga Center provides a supportive environment for people to shift to healthier lifestyles, improve their relationships, seek a higher level of self-fulfillment, and realize their full potential.

Dhyanalinga Yogic Temple

The Dhyanalinga is a powerful and unique energy form created by Sadhguru from the essence of yogic sciences. It is the first of its kind to be completed in more than two thousand years. The Dhyanalinga Yogic Temple is a meditative space that does not ascribe to any particular faith or belief system, nor does it require any ritual, prayer, or worship.

Within this architectural marvel, a dome structure without pillars, the energies of the Dhyanalinga seem to vibrate and allow even those unaware of meditation to experience a deep state of meditativeness, revealing the essential nature of life.

Every day, thousands of people converge at this unique meditation center to seek out inner peace and silence. As the focal point of Isha Yoga Center, the Dhyanalinga is rapidly gaining in its global reputation as being one of the most sought out places for meditation.

Isha Yoga Programs

Isha Yoga programs allow individuals to take tangible steps toward their inner growth. These programs are designed by Sadhguru as a rare opportunity for self-discovery under the guidance of a realized master.

An array of programs is conducted regularly by the foundation worldwide. These programs establish optimal health and vitality, provide enhanced mental calmness and clarity, and instill a deep sense of joy. They can be easily integrated into one's everyday life and embrace the human effort to reach inner awareness.

ACTION FOR RURAL REJUVENATION

A long-time vision of Sadhguru, Action for Rural Rejuvenation (ARR) is a pioneering social outreach program. ARR aims at providing comprehensive and ongoing rural rehabilitation services, such as free medical relief, yoga programs, nature awareness programs, and community games to the heart of the rural communities of India, creating an opportunity for villagers, including women and children, to take responsibility for their own lives and to restore and reach their ultimate well-being. So far, ARR has helped more than 1.7 million people in more than thirty-five hundred villages, in the southern states of India (as of July 2007). This initiative is also finding its way to the northwestern part of Africa.

ISHA VIDHYA

Isha Vidhya, an Isha Education Initiative, is committed to raising the level of education and literacy in rural India and to help disadvantaged children realize their full potentials. The project seeks to ensure quality education for children in rural areas in order to create equal opportunities for all to participate in and benefit from India's economic growth.

With English computer-based education complemented by innovative methods for overall development and blossoming of each individual, Isha Vidhya schools empower rural children to meet future challenges. Sadhguru's intention and goal is to start 206 English "computer friendly" matriculation schools within the next five to seven years, at least one in each *taluk* in Tamil Nadu. The schools are expected to benefit more than five hundred thousand students when fully functional.

PROJECT GREENHANDS

An inspiring ecological initiative of Isha Foundation, Project GreenHands seeks to prevent and reverse environmental degradation and enable sustainable living. The project aims to create 14 percent additional green cover in the state of Tamil Nadu in southern India. Drawing extensively on people's participation, 114 million trees will be planted statewide by the year 2010.

As a first step, a mass tree planting marathon was held on October 17, 2006. It resulted in 852,587 saplings being planted in 6,284 locations across twenty-seven districts in the state by more than 256,289 volunteers in just one day, setting a Guinness World Record.

ISHA REJUVENATION

Surrounded by thick forests at the tranquil foothills of the Vellingiri Mountains, Isha Rejuvenation helps individuals to experience inner peace and the joy of a healthy body. It offers a unique and powerful combination of programs, scientifically designed by Sadhguru, to bring vibrancy and proper balance to one's life energies. The programs contain a synthesis of *allopathic, ayurvedic,* and *siddha* treatments, and complementary therapies, along with the sublime wisdom of various ancient Indian sciences and spirituality. These treatments have had a phenomenal impact on the aging process and have led to miraculous recoveries from seemingly hopeless health situations.

All the proceeds of Isha Rejuvenation contribute toward providing free health care to rural villagers under the Action for Rural Rejuvenation initiative.

ISHA HOME SCHOOL

Isha Home School aims at providing quality education in a challenging and stimulating home-like environment. It is designed specifically for the inner blossoming and the well-rounded development of children.

With its prominent international faculty and Sadhguru's personal involvement in the curriculum, Isha Home School kindles the innate urge within children to learn and know. Focus is given to inculcating life values and living skills while maintaining the rigor of academic excellence as per national and international standards. It does not propagate any particular religion, philosophy, or ideology; rather, it encourages children to seek a deeper experience and inner understanding of the fundamentals of life.

ISHA BUSINESS

Isha Business is a venture that aims to bring a touch of Isha into the homes and environments of the community and to ultimately enrich people's lives. This opportunity is made available through numerous products and services, from architectural designs, construction, interior design, furniture design and manufacturing, landscape design, handicrafts and soft furnishings, to designer outfits from Isha Raiment.

All profits from this venture are used to serve the rural people of India through Isha Foundation's Action for Rural Rejuvenation initiative.

HOW TO GET TO ISHA YOGA CENTER

Isha Yoga Center is located thirty kilometers west of Coimbatore, at the foothills of Vellingiri Mountains, part of the Nilgiris Biosphere. Coimbatore, a major industrial city in South India, is well connected by air, rail, and road. All major national airlines operate regular flights into Coimbatore from Chennai, Delhi, Mumbai, and Bangalore. Train services are available from all the major cities in India. Regular bus and taxi services are also available from Coimbatore to Isha Yoga Center.

Visitors should contact Isha Yoga Center for availability and reservation of accommodations well in advance of arrival to the center, as they are generally fully booked.

CONTACT US

Isha Yoga Center
Semmedu (P.O.), Vellingiri Foothills
Coimbatore 641 114, India
Telephone: 91-422-2515345
E-mail: info@ishafoundation.org

Isha Institute of Inner Sciences
191 Anthony Dr.
McMinnville, TN 37110, USA
Telephone: 931-668-1900
E-mail: iiis@ishafoundation.org

Isha Institute of Inner Sciences
PO Box 559
Isleworth, TW7 5WR
United Kingdom
Telephone: 44-7956998729, 44-7939118981
E-mail: uk@ishafoundation.org

Website: www.ishafoundation.org

ABOUT THE AUTHORS

Cheryl Simone is a lifelong student of human potential, a spiritual seeker, an entrepreneur, a wife, a mother, and the CEO of several businesses. She lives in Atlanta, Georgia. She can be reached at cheryl.simone@yahoo.com.

For more information on Cheryl's experiences and to download a free introductory talk by Sadhguru entitled Inner Engineering, please log on to:

www.midnightswiththemystic.com

Sadhguru Jaggi Vasudev is a yogi, mystic, and visionary. He is a spiritual master with a difference. An arresting blend of profundity and pragmatism, his life and work serve as a reminder that inner sciences are not an esoteric discipline from an outdated past, but a contemporary science, vitally relevant to our times. Probing, passionate, and provocative, deeply insightful, devastatingly logical, and unfailingly witty, Sadhguru's talks have earned him the reputation of a speaker and opinion-maker of international renown.

With speaking engagements that take him around the world, he is widely sought after by prestigious global forums to address issues as diverse as human rights, business values, and social, environmental, and existential issues. He has been a delegate to the United Nations Millennium Peace Summit, a member of the World Council of Religious Leaders, and a special invitee to the Australian Leadership Retreat, the Tallberg Forum, and the World Economic Forum at Davos in 2006 and 2007. Listeners have been ubiquitously impressed by his astute and incisive grasp of current issues and world affairs, as well as his unerringly scientific approach to the question of human well-being.

Hampton Roads Publishing Company

. . . for the evolving human spirit

Hampton Roads Publishing Company
publishes books on a variety of subjects,
including spirituality, health, and other related topics.

For a copy of our latest trade catalog,
call toll-free, 800-766-8009,
or send your name and address to:

Hampton Roads Publishing Company, Inc.
1125 Stoney Ridge Road
Charlottesville, VA 22902
E-mail: hrpc@hrpub.com
Internet: www.hrpub.com